2

STORIES OF THE FIRST WORLD WAR

Jim Eldridge

■SCHOLASTIC

While the events described and some of the characters may be based on actual historical events and real people, the stories in this book are works of fiction.

Scholastic Children's Books
Euston House, 24 Eversholt Street,
London, NW1 1DB, UK
A division of Scholastic Ltd

London ~ New York ~ Toronto ~ Sydney ~ Auckland
Mexico City ~ New Delhi ~ Hong Kong

First published in the UK by Scholastic Ltd, 2014

Text copyright © Jim Eldridge, 2014
Foreword © Johnson Beharry, 2014
Cover background image of poppy field © Yolande de Kort/Trevillion Images

ISBN 978 1407 14055 1

All rights reserved
Printed and bound by CPI Group (UK) Ltd, Croydon, CR0 4YY

4 6 8 10 9 7 5 3

Papers used by Scholastic Children's Books are made from woods grown in sustainable forests.

To those who fell in the Great War, and all other conflicts.

Contents

Foreword

The Great War – as it was known at the time – was only supposed to last until Christmas of 1914, but ran almost until the end of 1918. Almost 15 million died or were injured during the War on the Western Front alone.

It's difficult to understand now what it would have been like to live through the First World War – this was a war that started with soldiers on horseback armed with swords and lances, and ended with tanks, planes and machine guns. When I joined the British Army at 18, I had little idea of the extent of what would be in store for me, but with television and news coverage of modern conflicts, I knew at least that I would be likely to face dangerous situations. Many young men and women – some as young as 13 – who volunteered or later conscripted to the armed forces in the 1914-1918 war, would have been horrified at what they found on the front lines. From the terrible conditions in the trenches to being attacked from the air – nothing like this had ever been seen before. More than 600 Victoria Crosses were awarded for acts of bravery during this war.

The stories in this book, told through the experiences of twelve young people, show how the First World War began, how it spiralled into the worst conflict the world had ever seen, and how, finally, it came to an end. A century on, the courage of people on the front lines, their friends and relatives at home, and the sacrifices they all made are truly moving.

Johnson Beharry, VC

Sergeant Johnson Beharry, VC, came to the UK from Grenada as a teenager and joined the British Army at the age of 21. He served in Northern Ireland and Kosovo before being posted to Iraq. He was awarded Britain's highest military honour – the Victoria Cross, or VC – in 2005, following two extraordinary acts of bravery in Iraq. He was the first to receive the honour in more than 20 years, and the first living person to be award the VC in over 49 years. Sergeant Beharry is still a member of the British Army, using his time to speak about his experiences with children and young people around the UK. He plans to work with young people in inner-city gangs to help them achieve happy, healthy lives, find work and escape the cycle of violence, drugs and poverty that can so badly affect their lives.

Introduction

The background to the First World War

On 4 August 1914, Britain declared war on Germany. For most people, this is the date that the First World War, also known as the Great War, started. But the roots of the First World War can be said to lie further back in history, in the Franco-Prussian War of 1870–1871, in which Prussia defeated France.

Prussia was a kingdom which had existed for many years, and during its war with France, Prussia joined with its allied states in Germany, to create a new and very large united German nation, which led to victory. In June 1888, the new ruler of this German state was Kaiser Wilhelm, King of Prussia, a grandson of Britain's Queen Victoria.

After being defeated by Germany in 1871, France was concerned that Germany might attack again and take further parts of the country. During the War, France had lost its regions known as Alsace-Lorraine to Germany.

Russia was also suspicious of Germany's ambitions to create a larger German Empire; so France and Russia signed an agreement which stated that if Germany attacked either country, then the other would offer military support.

There was no doubt that Germany was intent on enlarging its Empire. As early as 1905, Count Alfred von Schlieffen, then the Chief of German General Staff, had drawn up plans for attacks on both France and Russia. The Schlieffen plan was based on the opinion that Russia would be slower than France to deploy its troops in any German attack; and so Schlieffen proposed that Germany should make a lightning attack on France, and only when Germany had beaten France should Germany launch an attack on Russia.

The Schlieffen plan was developed by the German military and the German Government, to such an extent that by 1914, at the start of the War, Germany had assembled an army of over 4 million trained soldiers.

To secure its own borders against attack, Germany formed an alliance with neighbouring Austria-Hungary.

Germany had also been active in giving military support to the German colonists in South Africa during the Boer War against Britain (1899–1902). This prompted Britain to promise to side with France and Russia in the event of any military conflict with Germany in two agreements: the Entente Cordiale of 1904 (between Britain and France) and a similar understanding forged with Russia in 1907. At this time, Russia had a king – Tsar Nicholas (who was also a grandson of Queen Victoria).

So, by 1914, Europe was split into two camps, both suspicious of one another: Britain, France and Russia (the Allies) and Germany and Austria-Hungary (known as the Central Powers).

Each of these large nations had agreements and treaties with smaller nations, and it was an incident in one of these smaller nations that turned these rivalries into a full-scale world war.

In June 1914, Archduke Franz Ferdinand of Austria-Hungary, and his wife, Sophie, went on an official visit to Serbia; and on 28 June they were assassinated by Serbian anarchists in Sarajevo. As a result of this, on 28 July 1914, Austria-Hungary declared war on Serbia. Germany offered support in any conflict to its ally, Austria-Hungary.

Serbia appealed to its larger neighbour, Russia, for support as a fellow Slav state (the people came from the same ethnic Slav background). Germany warned Russia to keep out of any conflict. Russia refused, and made public its support for Serbia. As a result, Germany turned its warning into action and, on 1 August 1914, declared war on Russia.

This triggered Russia's defence treaty with France, and so, on 3 August, Germany declared war on France. The next day German troops attacked France, going through Belgium to do so. Belgium was a neutral country, but had a defence agreement with Britain, so when Germany attacked Belgium, on 4 August 1914, Britain – already committed to support France and Russia – declared war on Germany.

The First World War had begun in earnest.

The first British soldiers to go to fight in the War were those of the British Expeditionary Force. They embarked for France on 9 August and were sent to Mons in Belgium – just inside the Belgian border with France – to defend against the advancing German Army.

The BEF force of 80,000 men reached Mons on 21 August, to face an attacking German army of 160,000 men. In contrast to the style of warfare that dominated the Western Front later in the War (trenches, tanks, machine guns) many of these first encounters consisted of soldiers on horses, armed with swords and lances, and many on bicycles. In fact, the first British fatality of the War was a bicyclist, Private John Parr, a member of the British Bicycle Reconnaissance section of the BEF, who came up against a German unit near Obourg and was shot dead.

On 22 August the first British shot of the War in France was fired at Casteau, near Mons, by Edward Thomas, a cavalryman on patrol with the 4th Royal Irish Dragoons. The horse soldiers had entered the War.

Horses, swords, lances ...
and machine guns

24 August 1914

Fourteen-year-old Jules Bouchard and his best friend, Edgar Rhom, lay behind the grassy hillock, hidden from view.

"Let me have a turn!" whispered Edgar, desperate to get a look through the binoculars.

"In a second!" whispered Jules. "They're my binoculars, remember!"

In fact, officially they belonged to Jules's Uncle Maurice, who claimed that his brother Paul – Jules's father – had left them to him after he died. Jules had protested, and even angrily challenged his uncle to prove his claim to the precious binoculars. The result had been an angry outburst from Uncle Maurice, furious at Jules calling him a liar. Finally the priest had been called to intervene, pointing out that it had been a tense time for everyone, with poor Paul Bouchard killed by the Germans while defending his country, and this unhappy row was just an expression of the anguish the family was feeling.

Uncle Maurice had not been mollified, but he did his best to hide his hurt feelings. After all, it was the priest who had spoken.

For his part, Jules was not happy either. As far as he was concerned, his uncle had stolen the precious binoculars that should, by rights, have been his.

Eventually a compromise had been arrived at, again brokered by the priest, after urging from Jules's mother: Jules could borrow the binoculars from his uncle for one day a week, provided he always returned them in good condition.

Today was one of the days, and it was the day the British – who had arrived just a few days earlier – seemed to be making preparations to launch an attack against the despised Germans, the men who had murdered his father.

"Please, let me have a turn!" begged Edgar.

Reluctantly Jules handed the binoculars to Edgar, who pressed them to his eyes. From their position, they could see both camps, British and German, and both sets of cavalry; but they had chosen a spot nearer to the British camp, determined that if they were caught watching, they would be caught by the Allies, and not the hated Boche.

The sight of the British cavalry filled Jules with delight. They looked magnificent, with their superb tall horses, and the points of their lances glinting in the sun. And there were hundreds of them! Hundreds and hundreds!

They will smash the Boche! he muttered to himself. *They will go through the German ranks like knives through butter. They will drive them out. Belgium will be ours again, free from the hated enemy. The field would be soaked in German blood, and his father would be avenged!*

"What's happening?" he demanded. "Let me have them back!"

"I've only just started looking through them!" complained Edgar.

"Well, what can you see? Is anything happening? Are the soldiers getting on their horses yet?"

"The two with the most gold braid on their uniforms are talking," reported Edgar.

"Talking!" snorted Jules indignantly. "Why aren't they attacking?"

"I expect they're planning their attack," said Edgar. "Like I say, those two look like they're the ones in charge, so I think it'll be happening soon."

"Come on, you've had your turn!" said Jules impatiently. "Let me have a go!"

Edgar sighed and handed the binoculars back to Jules.

Jules pressed them to his eyes and focused on the two cavalrymen Edgar had described. Yes, they did look like officers, with the gold braid on their sleeves. These must be the men in charge. But what were they saying to one another?

"For heaven's sake, David, you know I'd follow you anywhere at any time, but this is suicide!"

Lieutenant-Colonel David Campbell looked coldly at his second-in-command and old comrade-in-arms, Archie Wilson.

"Suicide?" he mocked. "We are the 9th Lancers! That's what we do. We charge the enemy, lances and swords, and cut them down. How many times did we do it in South Africa against the Boers, winning each and every charge?"

9

"The Boers were farmers with single-shot rifles! These Germans are different."

"They are men on horses with lances and swords and revolvers – the same as us."

"And behind them are rows of German machine guns."

"They won't fire for fear of hitting their own men."

"And once we've gone through the Boche lines? What then?"

Campbell scowled, hesitated, then admitted: "Yes, all right, Archie. The same thought occurred to me, and I raised it with the Old Man. I suggested that after the first charge, once we've gone through the German lancers and we get near their guns, we ought to adopt the strategy Bob Baden-Powell's brought in for the 5th Dragoons: dismount and engage them with rifle fire."

"And what did he say?"

"What do you think? Virtually accused me of cowardice for even thinking about it. Started to blast me for sullying the image of the Lancers. 'The Lancers are horse soldiers, my boy! Honour the memory of the Charge of the Light Brigade!'"

Archie let out a sigh and shook his head.

"An unfortunate example," he said sourly. "As I recall, nearly all the Lancers were killed by the Russian guns in that particular charge."

"Yes, well, I started to make that point, but the Old Man just reminded me that I was an officer and that officers obeyed orders as well as soldiers."

The Old Man. The General.

That was one of the problems with the organization of this war, reflected Campbell. This was going to be a Modern War. There was talk of fast machine guns and aircraft; but over half of the Top Brass, the Field Marshals and Generals running the War on the Allies' side, were former cavalrymen and still thought of war as being waged by men on horses with swords and lances. Field Marshal John French, one of the two commanders of the British Expeditionary Force in France, was a former cavalryman with the 19th Hussars, and the other commander, Field Marshal Douglas Haig, had been a cavalryman in the 7th Hussars. To even suggest to these two men that cavalrymen fight on foot was seen as something "not done".

"What do the men say, Archie?" asked Campbell.

Archie shrugged.

"The men will follow you, sir, as they always have done. They believe in you." He gave a wry smile. "Some of them think you're a good-luck charm. Certainly the ones who were with us fighting the Boer. And that word spreads among the new chaps. So morale is high."

"Good," nodded Campbell. "In that case, better get them mounted up. An order is an order, and the sooner we get stuck into the Boche and show them we mean business, the better."

"And the German machine guns?"

"We put them out of action," said Campbell. "Cut down their gunners. Lances and swords, and revolvers. By the time we're through the German cavalry, with luck, the machine gunners won't have had time to get themselves organized."

Archie said nothing, but Campbell could tell from the look on his old pal's face that he felt this was highly unlikely, and he knew that Campbell felt the same way. The Germans were highly organized, highly trained. The machine gunners would be poised and waiting.

And first, they had to get past the German cavalry, the Uhlans, who proudly boasted they were the finest cavalry unit in Europe. Well, it was time to put that boast to the test.

"Orders are orders, Archie," said Campbell simply. "And this is war."

Archie snapped to attention and gave a sharp salute.

"Yes, sir!" he said briskly. "I'll prepare the men."

As Campbell watched Archie walk away, he remembered the previous times they'd ridden into battle together, in India, but mainly in South Africa against the Boers in the Boer War. And even then, that hadn't been a walkover. These so-called "Dutch farmers armed only with pitchforks and single-shot rifles" had held off the might of the British Army on more than one occasion. And now they were about to face the Uhlans, and then the guns.

Captain Walter Oberst stood surveying the scene through his field glasses. He was grateful he had decided to pay more money and buy the best field glasses: they afforded him a view of the British camp far away across the open ground, the fields, where he could see the British cavalry soldiers preparing their mounts.

"Captain!"

Oberst lowered his field glasses and turned to Leutnant Graf, who had appeared beside him and was standing as stiff as a ramrod, hand fixed to his temple in salute.

"At ease, Leutnant," said Oberst.

"Sir!"

Graf lowered his saluting arm, but he did not relax. *The Leutnant never relaxed*, thought Oberst. He was like a coiled spring, waiting for action.

"The Major's compliments, Captain. He reports that the machine gunners are in place and suggests that we mount up. He has received information that the British are preparing for a charge on our position."

Pompous idiot, thought Oberst. *"Received information" indeed!* One only had to take a look at the British camp through strong field glasses, as Oberst had done, and the evidence was there for all to see. But Major Clausen preferred to wait until he had "positive intelligence", which usually meant a carrier pigeon arriving with a note strapped to its leg from one of Clausen's spies, or a sighting from one of the aerial observer planes.

"Are the men ready?"

"They are, sir!"

"Then let us join them."

The men were, indeed, ready, standing stiffly to attention by their horses, dressed in their grey double-breasted tunics with the coloured plastron fronts, with a coloured sash over it, and their square-topped Polish-style lancer caps firmly on their heads. This had been the style of dress of the Uhlans in battle for centuries, as was the case with the lance that each man held, adorned with a small swallow-tailed flag just below the spearhead.

This is the way it should be, thought Oberst. *Armed horseback warrior against armed horseback warrior. We do not need these machine guns behind us. What use are they? They cannot fire while we are in front of them. They can only come into operation if the enemy make it through our ranks; and that will not happen, because we are Uhlan cavalry from Prussia, the finest of the finest.*

As Oberst headed towards his tent to put his precious field glasses away in a place of safety, he was surprised to see a staff car pull up beside Major Clausen. In the back of the car he could see the General. From the seat at the front next to the driver stepped Colonel Furstenwald. He spoke briefly to Major Clausen, who seemed momentarily stunned. Then he saluted, turned, and walked towards the line of machine guns behind the waiting cavalry horses and men.

Colonel Furstenwald then strode briskly towards Oberst.

"Captain!" he barked.

"Sir!" responded Oberst, snapping to attention and saluting.

"You will stand your men down," ordered the Colonel.

Oberst stood frozen, like a statue, his arm still in the stiff salute as he stared uncomprehendingly at the Colonel.

"Did you not hear me?" demanded Furstenwald.

"Stand … down?" repeated Oberst, like a man in a daze.

"Those are your orders," said Furstenwald. "Return them to the rear."

"But—" began Oberst.

The look on Furstenwald's face became icy.

"I said, those are your orders, Captain. Do not make me repeat them," he snapped, his tone threatening.

With that, Furstenwald saluted, turned on his heel and strode back to the staff car. He got in, and the car moved off, the engine roaring and popping.

Leutnant Graf, who had moved to a discreet distance upon the Colonel's arrival, appeared beside Oberst. He looked as bewildered as his captain.

"Did I hear the Colonel say the men were to stand down, Captain?" he said, puzzled.

Oberst turned and glared at the Leutnant. He should have barked at Graf for daring to eavesdrop on a conversation between superior officers, but he knew that he would be directing his anger at the wrong person.

"You did," he said, doing his best to keep his voice steady. "Stand them down, and return them to the rear of the machine-gun line."

"But—" began Graf, just as Oberst had done. The grim look on the Captain's face silenced him. He saluted.

"Yes, Captain."

Graf strode to the lines of waiting men and horses to give out the orders, while Oberst headed for his tent. He almost could not bring himself to watch as his beloved cavalry, the Uhlans, the pride of the German Army, were being forced to take a rear position behind the machine guns.

It was the end of the code of honour of the Warrior.

Mounted on their horses at the front of their troops, David Campbell and Archie Wilson studied the activity in the German camp through their binoculars.

"They're pulling the Uhlans out!" said Archie in surprise.

"That's what it looks like," agreed Campbell.

"Maybe they're going to put them in a side position," suggested Archie. "Ambush us."

"No," said Campbell, still watching. "They're moving them to the rear. Behind their machine guns."

"Moving the Uhlans to the rear!" said Archie, stunned. "But … why?"

"Because the Germans know the Lancers are the best," said Campbell aggressively. "They know their cavalry are no match for ours."

"It means we go straight up against their machine guns," said Archie, awed.

Campbell let out a heavy sigh.

"Yes," he said. "I suppose it does."

There was a silence between them, and then Archie said: "I don't suppose the Old Man will reconsider his decision about a mounted charge."

"No," said Campbell. "I don't think he will."

Archie turned in his saddle and looked at the rows of men behind them, sitting to attention on their horses, lances held ready, swords in scabbards at their sides. He turned back to Campbell.

"Well," he said, "I don't suppose they can shoot all of us at the first go. Some of us will get through." Then he grinned. "And we have got our lucky charm with us."

Campbell gave a wry grin. He looked at the sun glinting off the German machine guns in the far distance, then he raised his lance aloft, the small flag fluttering from just beneath the point.

"Lancers! Charge!" he shouted.

With that he dug his heels into the flanks of his mount, and they were off, the horses' hooves drumming against the hard ground as the hundreds of Lancers surged forward, lances held in one hand, reins in the other.

Edgar let out a gasp.

"They're attacking!" he said excitedly.

"What?" burst out Jules.

This time he didn't even ask, he reached out and snatched the binoculars from his friend and hastily pressed them to his eyes. Yes, the British cavalry were moving, and moving fast, the horses racing, some of the soldiers holding their lances pointed forward, others waving their swords in the air, while others pointed pistols straight ahead.

The German cavalry had retreated, gone to hide behind the line of machine guns.

Cowards! thought Jules angrily.

Everything was a blur of brown as the men in brown uniforms on mostly brown horses stampeded towards the German lines. The air was filled with the thunder of hooves, pounding, pounding, and the sound of horses breathing hard as they ran. And then there came a new sound, harsh, mechanical, deafening, even though it was farther away: clatter clatter clatter clatter clatter clatter…

And now the horses began to tumble. Not all of them. Some fell, some jumped over them and ran on. Men fell from their horses, crashed to the ground and stood up, only to be smashed with a hail of metal bullets from the German machine guns, making them twitch and jerk like marionettes, before crumpling to the earth, their blood staining the grass around them.

But still the horses came on, running, and now the soldiers were shouting and yelling as they waved their swords, heads down behind their horses' necks, but so many crashed down, somersaulted, crumpled to the ground in a broken heap, legs kicking and jerking, bodies writhing, the howls of horses in pain, the screams of men.

And still they ran on.

Jules lowered the binoculars. He felt sick.

"What's happening?" demanded Edgar.

"Nothing," said Jules hoarsely. "Nothing."

25 August–15 December 1914

On 24 August 1914, David Campbell led a charge by the 9th Lancers and 4th Dragoon Guards against German infantry and guns at Elouges in Belgium. It was just one part of the larger Battle of Mons, begun on 23 August, which was the first ground encounter between German and British forces.

The cavalry charge resulted in a loss to the British of 250 men and 300 horses. Campbell himself was wounded in the charge; but just two weeks later, on 6 September, he led another charge, this time against the German 1st Guard Dragoons, a lancer cavalry regiment. During this charge, Campbell was wounded by a lance in his shoulder, a sword wound to his arm, and a revolver wound in his leg. Despite these injuries, he survived and continued leading the cavalry throughout the First World War.

However, the role of the horse as an assault tactic was doomed against modern war machines, and the last mounted charge with horses was in 1917, when, on the orders of Field Marshal Haig, the Household Cavalry and the 10th Hussars launched an attack on the Hindenberg Line at Arras. The attackers were decimated by German machine-gun fire and barbed wire, and the 10th Hussars lost two thirds of their numbers.

As the months passed on the Western Front (as the area of France and Belgium where the two opposing armies met became known) the landscape and the nature of the War changed. The guns used by both sides became bigger, the shelling heavier. This led to the destruction of the massive and complex drainage system which had kept this area drained and useful for farming. With the drains broken and shattered, the clay became bog, areas of deep mud.

Defensive trenches that were dug by both sides soon filled with water. The addition of barbed wire and landmines as defences soon made the Western Front a hell-hole of mud and death.

Both sides tried to launch attacks, desperate to gain ground and push the enemy back. On 6 September came the First Battle of Marne, which lasted until 10 September. Then the Battle of Albert from 25 to 29 September, closely followed by the First Battle of Arras on 1 October. On 15 October the First Battle of Ypres began, which would last until 16 November. And each time the result was a virtual stalemate, with little ground gained, but with massive casualties – 25 per cent for each side at Marne, and at Ypres: 135,000 German casualties against 75,000 Allied.

On the Home Front, as well as fears about their men fighting in France and Belgium, there were also fears about a possible attack on Britain, especially of bombing raids conducted by the German airships known as Zeppelins. However, the first raids on Britain were made from the sea, by the German Navy. In November 1914, they launched an attack on the town of Great Yarmouth, on England's east coast.

Fortunately the town was untouched, with most of the shells falling onto the beach. Ships from the British Navy came to the town's defence, resulting in one British submarine and one German armoured cruiser being sunk.

On 16 December 1914, the defences of Britain's northern coastal towns were finally breached.

Bombardment!

16 December 1914

BOOOMMM!!!!! The force of the explosion threw ten-year-old Sally Moss into the road, tearing the skin of her knees on the uneven cobbles. A hail of bricks crashed to the ground around her. Miraculously, none of them hit her, though the dust filled her mouth and nose, choking her, and small chips of brick flew up and hit her from the force of the bricks smashing into the road.

Frantically, Sally pushed herself up off the ground and looked around for Billy, her little black-and-white dog, but he was nowhere to be seen.

Sally started to move towards a pile of smoking rubble lying half in the road, half on the pavement, terrified in case Billy was under it, when an explosion in the next street filled the air, sending a tremor through the ground with more smoke and dust billowing up.

"Sally!!"

The shout made her turn, and she saw Mrs Jenner, who lived next door to the grocer's shop, waving at her. "Come on! In our cellar!"

"I've got to find Billy!" Sally called back, and she started shouting again: "Billy! Billy!"

She found herself grabbed roughly by the arm.

"Stupid girl!" snapped Mrs Jenner. "You'll be killed out here!"

Mrs Jenner began to drag Sally towards her house.

"No!" begged Sally. "I have to find Billy!"

Just then there was another explosion, the force of it sending Sally lurching towards Mrs Jenner, who started running, dragging Sally with her. The next second they were stumbling through Mrs Jenner's doorway, just as there was a further explosion behind her, this one shaking the whole street, and for a moment Sally thought the house was going to come crashing down on them.

Mrs Jenner pushed open the small door under the stairs, grabbed Sally and roughly half-dragged the girl behind her down the narrow stairs, just as there was another massive BOOOOMMMMM!!!! from out in the street. The house shuddered and shook.

Sally stumbled down the stairs and into the cellar. Four children were already sitting on the floor – all of them looking terrified. Sally recognized them: Mrs Jenner's two sons, Eric and Walter, twins, aged eight, and Mary and Betty Wisdom, the daughters of the sweet-shop owner next door. Mary was six, and Betty was ten, and in the same class as Sally at school.

Sally was suddenly aware that she was still holding the small milk churn her mother had given her to get some milk from Hampden's Dairy. She'd never made it. The small metal milk churn was still empty. And Billy was gone.

"Sit down," Mrs Jenner commanded, settling herself on a pile of sacks in one corner.

"I have to find Billy," repeated Sally, as if in a daze. Everything had happened so quickly. One moment she was walking along the street, milk churn in one hand and Billy on his lead in the other, the next, there had been a loud whizzing sound in the air. She'd looked up and seen a large shining object flying through the sky, coming from the direction of the sea, which lay just a few streets away from where she stood.

Mrs Jenner shook her head.

"If you go out there now you'll be killed," she said. "We're being bombed. The buildings are falling down." Then, as if to reassure Sally, she added: "Billy will be safe. He'll find somewhere to hide. Dogs always do."

No, they don't, thought Sally. *Dogs are stupid. They panic and run out in the road and get killed, like her gran's dog, Buster, did.*

"She's odd," said Betty, looking accusingly at Sally. "Ever since her daddy went off to war she's been strange."

"Shush!" said Mrs Jenner sharply.

"Well it's true," said Betty defiantly. "She acts like she's not here."

But I am here, thought Sally. *I don't want to be, but I am.*

From above, there was another crashing explosion, and once again the house shook. Even here in the cellar, it felt as if the walls were going to come down on them.

"Sit down!" barked Mrs Jenner. "We'll go out and look for him when it stops."

Reluctantly Sally sat down on the damp floor. The cellar was lit by three candles, which threw an eerie glow on the brick walls.

24

Mary Wisdom suddenly began to cry.

"We're going to die!" she whimpered.

"No you're not," said Mrs Jenner firmly, although Sally heard the tremor in the woman's voice and realized: *She's afraid as well. We are all going to die.*

"Grandad said this wouldn't happen," said Betty, upset and angry. "He said we were too far away here in Yorkshire for the German planes to reach us and bomb us. He said their planes couldn't carry enough petrol to reach Scarborough."

"It's not planes," piped up Eric. *Or was it Walter?* wondered Sally. The twins looked so alike, it was hard to tell who was who.

"Well, Grandad said the Zeppelins wouldn't be able to get here either," continued Betty, still upset at having been lied to by her grandfather. "He said our fighter planes would shoot them down."

"It's n-not Zeppelins either," said the other twin, and Sally realized that this one was Eric. She recognized his slight stammer, and wondered why one twin had a stammer when his identical twin didn't.

"They're German battleships," added Walter. "Our Joe said he thought he saw them."

Joe was the twins' older brother, aged fourteen.

"Battleships?" echoed Sally.

"B-big ones," nodded Eric. "F-four of them. He went off to find someone to tell." Sally shot a look at Mrs Jenner, doing her best to try and appear calm, but from the way she twisted the hem of her dress between her hands, and bit her lip, Sally knew that the woman was thinking of her son, Joe, and wondering where he was, and if he was safe; just the same as she was terrified for Billy.

So, they sat in the cellar. Sally knew that Mrs Jenner was right – there was nothing else they could do while the bombs and shells rained down on them.

Is this how it is in France for my daddy? she thought.

Her daddy had gone off to fight in the War. Six weeks ago she and her mum had waved him goodbye as he caught the bus to the training ground. Since then they'd had letters from him once a week for the two weeks he was training, and only one letter since he'd left for France. That letter had been three weeks ago. It hadn't said much, just that he loved them and was thinking of them, and he hoped he'd be back with them at their house in Inkerman Street in Scarborough soon.

Since then, there'd been nothing from him – no letters, no postcards, no messages.

Sally had heard stories of what things were like at The Front: the trenches filled with water, the barbed wire, the shells from the big guns coming down on them.

Was it the same for her daddy as it was for her and the others right now? Was he sitting in a trench while bombs and shells fell exploding around him?

Was he even alive?

She shut her eyes and tried to blot out the image of him, lying dead in a trench, which had filled her thoughts so often since they'd had that last letter.

"I don't want you to go," she'd said to him just before he left to catch the bus.

"I have to, my love," he'd replied. "It's war. We all have to do our duty. Yours is to stay here and look after your mum. Will you do that?"

"Yes," she'd said. And she bit her lip to stop herself crying as her daddy kissed her on her forehead. Then he gave Mum a big hug, and walked off to the waiting bus.

Outside, the shelling continued, the house shaking with each new explosion. Sally was amazed that it hadn't come down on them. With each new BANG!!! she expected bricks to fall off the walls, or the wooden timbers that held the floor up above them to collapse.

She wasn't sure how long they sat there. Mary Wisdom was still crying. Betty, instead of being sympathetic, barked at her little sister angrily, "For heaven's sake, shut up!"

"She can't help it," said Mrs Jenner. "She's frightened."

"I'm frightened, but I don't cry!" said Betty. "She's just making it worse for us!"

"I w-wonder where Joe is?" said Eric suddenly, and he began to cry.

Unlike Betty, Walter put his arm around his brother and cuddled him to him.

"He'll be all right," said Walter, his voice shaky. "Joe's always all right."

"Yes, Joe's always all right," said Mrs Jenner in a terrified whisper.

They sat, listening and waiting. Mary's whimpers could be heard when there were lulls in the shelling. And finally there was silence.

"It's stopped," said Walter.

"I can go out and look for Billy," said Sally, getting up.

"No, not yet!" said Mrs Jenner, leaping to her feet and moving to block the way to the stairs. "They might start again!"

Sally hesitated, then waited. She stood there, waiting for Mrs Jenner to move away from the stairs, but Mrs Jenner didn't.

"I have to go," appealed Sally.

"Not yet," said Mrs Jenner.

The children looked at Mrs Jenner, unsure of what was going on.

"It's st-stopped," said Eric. "The sh-shelling's stopped."

"I think we should wait," said Mrs Jenner.

Sally looked at her. There was something odd in the way she spoke. It wasn't as if she was afraid there would be more bombing, it was more of what she was afraid of finding when she went back up to the street.

She doesn't want to go out and find Joe dead, Sally realized.

"I'm going!" said Sally. "I have to go home and see my mum and let her know I'm all right!"

It was a lie, she was going to look for Billy, but she knew that saying she was going home was a harder thing for Mrs Jenner to argue against. While Mrs Jenner struggled to come up with another argument, Sally dodged round her and bolted for the stairs.

"It's still dangerous!" Mrs Jenner called desperately after her, but Sally had gone, already halfway up the stairs. Behind her, she heard Betty Wisdom say, "I'm staying here! I don't want to be killed!"

Sally opened the front door and stepped out into the street, and stopped, shocked.

It was as if the whole street had been picked up and then smashed down by some enormous angry giant. The road was filled with rubble, cobbles, sand, dirt, just lifted up and scattered.

The house directly opposite Mrs Jenner's was ... gone. Mr and Mrs Miller's house. Where it had stood there was now just a gaping hole, with the houses on either side leaning dangerously in to the gap where the house had once been. Smoke rose from the rubble where the Millers' house had stood.

Household items and personal things were scattered around the rubble-strewn street. An upturned pram lay in the road. A pink baby's bootee. A framed photograph of a family, smiling at the camera, only the glass was broken and the frame smashed.

Further along, a window frame lay in the road, with net curtains still attached.

As Sally walked, she saw other things: a rag doll lay on a smouldering door. The door was scorched and burnt, and the rag doll was on fire, flames catching on the doll's woollen hair.

A foot was poking out from a pile of bricks. It looked as if a wall had fallen down and hit someone. As she got nearer she saw the foot had a woman's shoe on it, and there was a hand also poking out. The hand had a wedding ring on one of the fingers.

I wonder who it is, she thought.

She'd seen a dead person before – her grandad – but that had been different. He'd been in his coffin, and the family had come along to look at him and pay their respects before his funeral. Her dead grandad had been wearing his suit, and a collar and tie. The thing was, the body in the coffin had *looked* like her grandad, but at the same time it hadn't. It was as if someone had made a waxwork of her grandad and put it in the wooden box.

The woman lying hidden under the pile of bricks looked real, even if Sally could only see her foot and one hand. Sally wondered if she was still alive, but then she saw the trail of dark red blood, sticky and drying on the road, and knew she wasn't. The woman was dead.

Sally looked along the street. No one else was out yet, she was the only one.

"Billy!" she called, and then again, her voice more desperate this time: "Billy!!!!"

She listened, hoping to hear an answering bark, but there was nothing.

She heard other sounds, people calling, their voices despairing, calling for help. Then there was the sound of footsteps, at first shuffling, and then running.

A policeman appeared. He looked shaken. "Are you all right?" he asked.

"Yes," said Sally. She pointed to the woman buried beneath the pile of bricks. "There's a woman there. She's hurt."

The policeman hurried to where Sally was pointing. He lifted the woman's hand, and checked her pulse. He let the hand drop down again, and he got up, shaking his head.

"She's dead." He gestured towards the holes where buildings had stood. "They're all dead."

He's in shock, realized Sally. *Everyone's in shock. We're all…*

Alive, was the word that struck her. *We're alive, and lots of people are dead.*

"I've lost my dog," she said. "He's black and white. He answers to the name of Billy. Have you seen him?"

The policeman looked at her as if she was mad.

"A dog?" he said.

"Yes," said Sally. "He ran away when the first bomb went off."

The policeman shook his head.

"I haven't got time to look for a dog!" he said. "There are people dead! People missing! And you should go home! Where is your home?"

"Inkerman Street," said Sally.

The policeman nodded.

"They missed Inkerman Street," he said. "Go home."

"I have to find Billy," insisted Sally.

"Go home!" said the policeman, louder this time, and Sally heard anger in his voice which he was trying hard to keep under control; and she thought with alarm: *he might take me home and hand me over to my mum. If he does that, she won't let me go out again to look for Billy. Or the policeman might arrest me and take me to the police station.*

"I'll go home," she nodded.

At least she knew her mum was all right. The German shelling hadn't hit Inkerman Street.

Sally walked away from the policeman. She could feel his eyes on her, watching her, but then she heard someone shouting for help and she turned to see the policeman hurry off towards the frightened voices.

I must find Billy, she thought. *He'll be scared. He could be trapped.*

She turned and began to walk back the way she'd originally been walking, along the rubble-strewn street, past collapsed buildings, and suddenly, she felt overwhelmed by it all. It was as if she had been keeping it at bay, pretending none of it had happened, but now as she looked around her at the horror, it hit her, and she crumpled down on to the ground and began to cry as the images filled her mind – the dead woman's foot sticking out of the pile of bricks, her dead hand with the wedding ring on it, the Millers' house gone, the upside-down pram, the pink baby's bootee, the rag doll burning on the scorched door, the piles of smouldering rubble, the look of agony and fear on Mrs Jenner's face, the sound of the shells crashing down and exploding, the sound filling her mind, deafening her even though they were now gone – and she sobbed. She could hear herself wailing.

"Daddy!" she howled. "I want my daddy!"

She hunched over, her head in her hands, sobbing, her body heaving as she poured out her shock and misery in tears…

And then she felt a nudging at her elbow. She put out a hand to push whoever it was away, and her hand felt something wet; something … familiar.

She looked, and saw Billy, standing looking at her, his big brown eyes worried as he pushed his nose at her elbow, then into her side. His lead was still attached to his collar and trailing on the ground.

"Billy!"

She grabbed him round the neck with both arms and hugged him to her.

"You're safe!" she whispered.

But Billy backed away from her and barked. Sally looked at him, baffled. What was up with him? Why wasn't he licking her face, which is what Billy usually did when she came home after school, keen to show her he was pleased to see her?

Billy barked again, backing away from her. Then he moved towards her, still barking, but once again he backed away from her.

He wants to show me something, realized Sally. She stood up, and immediately Billy ran off. But then he stopped and stood, barking at her. He waited until Sally had reached him, but just as he was about to bolt off again, Sally reached down and grabbed the end of his trailing lead.

"Right!" she said. "Show me!"

Billy began to run, straining against the lead, pulling Sally along behind him, his nose close to the ground as he followed a scent. They ran past fallen buildings and more piles of smouldering rubble, more scenes of devastation, until Billy stopped by the remains of a bombed-out house. He began scrabbling and digging with his front paws at a crushed and broken door, and as he did so, Sally heard a faint call from beneath: "Help! Is someone there?"

Sally looked around for someone to help her, but there was no one in the street – all the rescuers were busy elsewhere.

"Yes!" Sally called out. "I'm here! Wait!"

She took hold of the edge of the broken door and tried to raise it, but it wouldn't lift. Then she realized why: broken bricks and rubble were lying on the top half of the door, adding to the weight.

She shuffled on to the door and began to push the rubble off it. Finally the door was clear, and this time when she put her fingers beneath the edge and tried to lift it, it moved, and then rose a bit. She slid the door along as far as she could and then let it drop down. Sally saw that it had exposed a hole beneath, one that went down, and from the smell she realized that a drain had been exposed, and covered with the door and bricks and rubble when the house nearby had been blown up.

"Hello!" she called, and she peered down into the narrow gap that led down to the drain. Someone was down there, caught in the tiny space, trapped, and Sally was stunned when the person called her name: "Is that you, Sally Moss?"

It was Joe Jenner.

"Yes," she said. "Are you hurt?"

"No," said Joe. "I got blown down this hole, and then all that stuff came down on top of it. I can't get out. The walls are too high and too slippery for me to get a grip."

"I've got an idea," said Sally.

She whistled Billy over, then took off his lead. She fixed one end of it to the door handle of the broken door, and let the rest of the lead dangle down into the hole.

"Is that any good?" she asked.

"Perfect!" said Joe.

He reached up, grabbed the end of the dog lead, and then began to climb up, pressing the soles of his boots against the wall. He slipped a few times, but finally he reached the top, and hauled himself out of the hole.

He stood surveying the devastation around him, while Sally untied the dog lead from the door handle and put it back on Billy's collar.

"The Germans have destroyed the town," said Joe, shocked. "There must be hundreds dead."

"Your mum and brothers are safe," said Sally. "I was with them in your cellar."

Joe nodded.

"I'll go and tell them I'm all right," he said. "And you've got to come with me, Sally. My mum will be angry if you don't, she'll want to say thank you for saving me."

"I didn't save you. Billy did," said Sally.

"Billy found me first, but you saved me," said Joe.

Sally shook her head.

"I can't. I've got to get to my house," she said. "Mum will be worried."

"You've got to go past our house to get to yours," insisted Joe. "It'll only take a second."

Sally hesitated. Joe was right, she had to go past Mrs Jenner's house to get back to Inkerman Street, and this way she could show Mrs Jenner she'd found Billy, and it was Billy who'd found Joe, and that Billy wasn't a stupid dog.

"All right," she said.

They ran, all three: Joe, Sally and Billy, driven now to get home and let their families know they were alive and safe.

Mum will kill me, thought Sally. *I should have gone straight home after I left Mrs Jenner's.*

But then she told herself: *but if I had, I wouldn't have found Billy, and Joe would have still been stuck down there in that drain and could have starved to death.*

As they neared the destruction outside the Jenners', Sally saw that there was a crowd gathered in the street in front of the house, and among them she saw her mum.

"Mum!" she called.

Mrs Moss turned at the sound of Sally's shout and glared angrily at her daughter.

"Sally! You naughty girl! I've been worried sick!"

"I was looking for Billy," defended Sally.

"Joe!!"

The yell of delight and relief burst out from Mrs Jenner, and then she was running towards Joe, with Eric and Walter running close behind. Mrs Jenner grabbed Joe.

"I thought you were dead!" she said, hugging him tight.

"Sally found me," said Joe.

"Billy found him," corrected Sally.

Sally's mum stood, torn between a mixture of hurt and anger that Sally had gone off instead of coming home, and relief at finding her alive and safe. Then she ran forward and scooped Sally up in her arms.

"I thought *you* were dead, too!" she whispered.

And Sally realized her mum was crying.

"I'm all right, Mum," she said. "And I found Billy."

Mrs Moss released her and wiped her eyes on her sleeve. Then she produced a small crumpled brown envelope from her coat pocket.

"The postman came just after you left to get the milk," she said. She smiled through her tears and thrust the envelope at Sally. "It's from your dad. He's all right. And he's put a separate one in there for you."

Sally took the envelope and looked at it as if it was the most precious thing in the world – which it was.

Sally's mum looked at where the Jenners were still engrossed in talking to Joe, fussing over him, making sure he wasn't injured. Then she looked around at the carnage and destruction.

"I have to do something, Sally," she said, her voice suddenly determined. "We've still got each other, and we've still got Dad, even though he's in France, and Mrs Jenner has still got her boys. But some people have lost everything today: their houses, everything they own, and…" her voice dropped as she said sadly, "people they loved."

By now more rescuers had appeared: policemen, firemen, nurses from the hospital, going from pile of rubble to pile of rubble, searching for anyone they might be able to save.

"You go home, Sally, and take Billy with you," said Mrs Moss. "I'm going to help. I can do bandaging. I can look after people." She shook her head. "People are going to need help now, Sally."

"I can help," said Sally. "I got Joe Jenner out of that hole."

Mrs Moss looked as if she was going to shake her head, but then she nodded.

"You're right. You did. Come on then. Let's go and do our bit. We'll show the Hun that it's not just our soldiers who can't be beaten by them. The same goes for the women and children!"

17 December–24 December 1914

The attack on Scarborough, Hartlepool and Whitby from the sea by battlecruisers and destroyers of the German Navy killed 137, with a further 592 casualties. It was seen as a humiliation for British Intelligence, which had failed to realize the attack was about to happen. This was despite British codebreakers having got hold of German codebooks from sunk or captured German vessels, and being aware on the evening of 14 December that a German battlecruiser squadron would shortly be leaving port. It was also seen as a humiliating defeat for the British Navy, which failed to intercept the German ships on their way to the North Yorkshire coast; and also failed to catch the German ships as they headed back to Germany after the attack on the Yorkshire towns.

Meanwhile, on the Western Front, a stalemate had developed. Both sides had dug in for the winter, and the deep German and Allied trenches stretched all the way from the Swiss border northwards to the border between France and Belgium.

The trenches that housed the British troops were particularly wet. The soldiers put down wooden walkways, known as duckboards, in the trenches to try to keep from sinking into the mud and clay; but this did not stop them from getting "trench foot". This was a disease caused by their feet being permanently soaked in water and mud. "Trench foot" caused soldiers' feet to swell, and often, once they'd taken their boots off, they found their feet had swollen so much they couldn't put their boots back on again.

As winter drew on, it looked as if it was going to be a miserable, and deadly, Christmas for both sides.

Football truce

24 December 1914

Fifteen-year-old Edwin Parsons peered over the edge of the trench towards the German lines. Officially, he shouldn't even be here fighting in the trenches, but like many boys he'd lied about his age when he'd gone to volunteer at the Recruiting Office back home in Walsall. Not the first time he'd gone there, though. The first time, when the Sergeant in the Recruiting Office had asked him how old he was, he'd answered truthfully: "Fourteen."

The Sergeant had given him a kindly apologetic smile and said, "Sorry, son, you're too young. Come back again when you're eighteen." And then the Sergeant had winked and grinned broadly as he whispered, "Tomorrow, eh?"

Sure enough, the next day Edwin returned to the Recruiting Office and encountered the same Sergeant, and when he asked him, "How old are you?" Edwin had replied, "Eighteen."

"Perfect!" the Sergeant had beamed. "Welcome to the Army, and your chance to fight for King and Country!"

When Edwin returned home that afternoon and told his mother he'd volunteered, she burst into tears and begged him not to go. Her brother, Edwin's Uncle Morton, on the other hand, looked at Edwin proudly, saluted him, and said, "Well done, Edwin! If I was a younger man and didn't have my injury, I'd be going myself!"

Actually, Edwin – along with the rest of the family – wasn't quite sure what Uncle Morton's injury actually *was*. Sometimes it was his back, sometimes it was an arm, and then it often seemed to be a leg that prevented him doing much. Especially work. Uncle Morton had been known to start a job, under pressure from others, or lack of ready money, but very soon his "injury" would surface and he'd be "forced to leave".

As for being "too old to join the Army", Edwin was sure that Uncle Morton was younger than some of the men he knew who'd volunteered.

All of this meant that Edwin didn't really have much time for Uncle Morton's opinion of him as a "brave volunteer", but he did worry about his mother. She was a widow, and Edwin was her only source of income. Since he'd left school six months previously, he'd regularly handed his mother his weekly pay packet, and she gave him enough for his needs. He was fairly sure she was saving the rest, rather than spend it, because her clothes were never new, and she seemed to eat very little.

I wonder how she is? he thought to himself. He looked up at the sky and hoped that she was looking up at this same sky, seeing the same as he was. *Dear God,* he prayed silently, *please look after my mum.*

His thoughts were interrupted by the arrival of Chalky, one of the soldiers he'd grown close to since he'd been out in the trenches. Chalky was in his late twenties and had taken it upon himself to become a father figure to Edwin.

"What's up?" asked Chalky.

Edwin pointed and whispered. "Those lights."

Chalky shook his head.

"The Boche are taking a chance," he muttered.

Chalky was referring to the Rule of Three, as they called it in the trenches. A naked light in a trench in the dark could give away a soldier's position to an enemy sniper. And the longer a match remained lit, the more chances a sniper would have to get a good aim for his shot. With matches in short supply in the trenches, especially dry matches in the wet conditions, a soldier striking a match in order to light his damp cigarette would usually offer the same lit match to a comrade, and then to another before the match burnt out. Until the soldiers realized that by the time the third soldier accepted the lighted match, any watching sniper had got the range and distance for his shot, and that third soldier often died with a bullet through his head. For that reason, soldiers usually kept a hand over a lighted match when lighting a cigarette or a pipe, to keep the light hidden.

Not that Edwin was affected by that. He didn't smoke, and he had no intention of ever doing so. It was smoking that had killed his father. Lung cancer, emphysema and bronchitis. His father's death had been slow and miserable; he'd wasted away before the eyes of the family. The big, strong man that Edwin had remembered when he was growing up had become a thin, shrivelled bag of bones, light enough for Edwin to carry on his own when they'd taken him to the hospital that last time.

Not that the hospital had been able to do much. In fact, they'd sent him home after two days.

"There's nothing more we can do for him," the doctor had told Edwin's mother. "You're throwing away good money by keeping him here. You can't afford it, and we can't afford him occupying a bed."

And so they'd carried him home again, and he'd died a week later.

Smoking kills, thought Edwin. *And war kills*. For six weeks he'd been out here, and all that time the dead had piled up around him: some shot by snipers; some killed during attacks launched across No Man's Land towards the German lines; some cut down in a hail of machine-gun bullets, or left to dangle on barbed wire.

The Germans died, too. There were plenty of bodies still lying in No Man's Land between the British and German front lines, slowly rotting, the putrid smell sweeping back across to Edwin and his comrades when the wind changed direction. The rats fed on them, of course, and grew fat. Edwin didn't think he'd ever seen rats as big as the ones out here: huge bloated rats almost as big as cats.

His thoughts were suddenly interrupted by a low whistle of surprise from Chalky.

"Those ain't matches you can see, Edwin," he whispered. "They're candles." He frowned, puzzled. "Why are the Germans putting candles along the edge of their trench? Think it's some kind of trick?"

And then they heard it, low at first, but getting louder: the sound of men singing. And not the usual rousing marching songs the Germans sometimes sang, or the German national anthem, but this was a familiar song.

"I know that!" exclaimed a voice behind them, and Edwin saw they'd been joined by Jim Haddock, a soldier in his twenties, like Chalky. "That's a Christmas carol we sing at home. But they're singing different words."

"It's German," said Edwin.

They listened, and the words floated across to them.

"*O tannenbaum, O tannenbaum,*
Wie treu sind deine Blätter..."

"Bloody cheek!" snorted Haddock. He scowled. "I'll soon show 'em the proper words!"

With that, Haddock began to sing, to the same tune:

"O Christmas tree, O Christmas tree!
Your branches green delight us!"

The singing from the German trenches suddenly stopped. Haddock chuckled.

"There!" he said. "That sorted them out!"

There was a pause, and then they heard a cautious shout from the German lines that echoed eerily towards them.

"Hey, Tommy! You know our carol, *ja*?"

"I know it all right," shouted back Haddock indignantly, "but it's *our* carol, not yours!"

There was another pause, and then the same voice called back: "It was composed by a German!"

"Nonsense!" called back Haddock. "My Aunt Freda in Southend used to sing it to me."

There was another pause, then another voice called out: "I, too, have an Aunt Frieda."

"What, in Southend?" demanded Haddock, puzzled.

"*Nein*, in Bavaria," called back the voice. "She is married to my Uncle Heinrich. Heinrich and Frieda from Bavaria."

"Well my Aunt Freda's married to my Uncle Henry!" called back Haddock defiantly.

"Careful," said Chalky warningly to Haddock. "We don't want to be giving the enemy information about ourselves. Remember what the officers said, they might use it against us."

"How is the fact that I've got an Uncle Henry and an Aunt Freda in Southend going to help the enemy?" demanded Haddock.

"I think Heinrich is German for Henry," said Edwin. He smiled. "So you and him have got something in common, you've both got an Uncle Henry and an Aunt Freda."

"We've got another thing in common," muttered Haddock sourly, "we're both freezing our socks off in a perishing cold wet trench."

"Hey, Tommy!" called the German voice.

"What?" called back Haddock.

"Careful," urged Chalky again, an note of warning in his voice. "It could be a trick. They could be lining up where we are by the sound of your voice."

"They know where we are," countered Haddock. "We're in the same

46

place we've been for the past two months. In this bloody cold trench, just the other side of No Man's Land."

"Hey, Tommy!" came the call from the German again.

"What?" called Haddock again.

"You know any good Christmas songs?"

"Of course we do!" retorted Haddock. "And proper ones with proper English words!" And he began to sing:

"Good King Wenceslas looked out

On the feast of Stephen!

When the snow lay round about, deep and crisp and even!"

"Ha!" came the shout from the German lines. "That is also a German carol!"

"Rubbish!" roared back Haddock, his voice full of indignation.

"What's going on, Private Haddock?" demanded a voice.

Edwin, Chalky and Haddock turned round and found themselves looking into the face of Lieutenant Pennant, their immediate commanding officer. Behind him stood half-a-dozen other soldiers from their regiment, all with the same puzzled expression on their faces.

"Er..." began Haddock awkwardly. The same voice as before called from the German lines.

"Well, Tommy? Do you have a song for Christmas that isn't a German one?"

This was followed by the sound of mocking laughter, at which Haddock's scowl deepened.

"It's the Boche, sir," he explained to Lieutenant Pennant. "They started singing Christmas carols."

"And they've stuck candles along the edge of their trench," put in Chalky.

Pennant peered over the top of the trench, and then ducked down again.

"So I see," he said.

"Well the thing is, sir," continued Haddock. "They keep insisting that all our carols are German."

"What?!" demanded one of the newly arrived soldiers, a large Welshman called Dewey. There was no mistaking the outrage in his voice.

"German!"

"That's what he said," nodded Haddock.

"Well we'll give them one that's definitely not German!" snorted Dewey. He turned to his fellow soldiers and said: "Come on men: '*Ar Hyd y Nos*'!"

And Dewey and the men with him began to sing, a song that Edwin recognized as one he had sung himself often at Christmas time, at church and at home: "All Through the Night". But the language that Dewey and his friends were singing in was not English, and neither was it German. It was a language unfamiliar to Edwin, melodic, beautiful, haunting, and as he listened to the men sing *"Holl amrantaur ser ddywedant, Ar hyd y nos"* the English words he was familiar with ran through his mind: "Sleep my child and peace attend thee, All through the night."

When Dewey and his comrades had finished, the silence hung in the air for a good few minutes. Suddenly it was broken by the sound of clapping from the German lines, and then a voice called out, "That is a good carol, Tommy! And you sing it well!"

Then another voice called, "Do you play football as well as you sing?"

"Better!" called back Haddock.

"No," growled Dewey. "We sing best!"

"He's talking to me," snorted Haddock to Dewey. "And I play football better than I sing."

"I should hope so," said one of Dewey's squad. "My dog sings better than you."

Haddock was just about to retort to this insult, when the German called out: "Then what say we play a game tomorrow? See which is the better team!"

"A football game for Christmas Day!" called out another German.

Haddock looked at Lieutenant Pennant.

"What do you say, Lieutenant?" he asked, and his tone was excited. "Play the Boche at football and beat 'em! Put 'em in their place! Show 'em who's boss!"

Pennant looked sceptical.

"Well, I'm not sure what HQ might have to say about it," he said thoughtfully.

"If we beat them, HQ will be delighted!" said Haddock enthusiastically.

"*If*," echoed Pennant doubtfully.

"Oh come on, sir!" appealed Haddock. "These are Germans. We *invented* football! There's no way they can beat us!"

"We've got Henry Butt in the squad," said Chalky. "He used to play for Arsenal before the War."

"And I played a bit back in Wales," said another of Dewey's singing pals.

"Ivor was an international!" nodded Dewey. "Played against England!"

"There you are, sir!" urged Haddock. "It'll be a *British* team!"

"Well, Tommy?" called the voice from the German lines. "What do you say?"

"Or are you scared?" laughed another voice. "Afraid we will beat you!"

"Never!" roared Haddock.

He turned back to Pennant, who asked: "Do we think we'll have eleven men who'd be prepared to go out into No Man's Land and risk the fact that it might be a trick?"

"Yes, sir!" nodded Haddock. "Me, for one!"

"And me," added Ivor.

"I'll do it," said Edwin, and he was surprised to hear himself volunteering, and for such a mad idea. A football match between two deadly enemies in the middle of a war!

"Very well," nodded Pennant. "But we have to win!"

Haddock grinned broadly.

"You leave it to us, sir!" he said. "I'll draw up the team tonight!"

Christmas Day, thought Edwin, looking around him at the barbed wire, the trenches, the sandbags, and the thin wisps of cold mist that hung over the makeshift pitch that had been cleared in No Man's Land, as he and the rest of the team, and their soldier-supporters, waited for the Germans to appear from their lines.

"Maybe they ain't coming?" muttered Ivor Evans, standing in the makeshift football strip of khaki army shirt, uniform trousers, and heavy army boots that all the team wore.

"They'll be here," said Chalky. He pointed towards the German line, where a white flag of truce had been fixed to a post and was fluttering in the wind. "They're just trying to get an advantage by making us wait in the cold."

"I said we should've worn our greatcoats," complained Henry Butt.

Edwin slapped his arms to warm himself up. He couldn't get over the strange feeling of excitement at what was about to happen: a football match between the British and German sides in the middle of a war.

He wondered what they'd say back home in Walsall when he wrote to them about this, if the censors allowed him to write that, of course. There seemed to be so many things that soldiers weren't allowed to write about in their letters home: the weather, the rats, the fighting. He thought of them back home on this day. His mum would be round at Gran and Grandad's, along with Uncle Morton, and various uncles and aunts and cousins and nieces and nephews. Auntie Beryl would play a few uplifting Christmas hymns on the piano, and everyone would obediently sing along with them. And then Uncle Peter would take over and the piano keys would be thumped heartily as he played cheerful favourites like "Roll out the Barrel", as well as jaunty Christmas songs about Santa and snowmen.

He looked around at the rest of the British team standing with him, most of them jumping up and down to keep out the cold. Jim Haddock had appointed himself captain for the occasion; then there was the Welsh international Ivor Evans, Henry Butt, the former Arsenal player, Dinny Morris, Ewan Mars, Bill Kidman, Albert Oliver, Jack Lee, Edgar Field, and, towering over the rest of the team, the tall figure of Percy Smith, the goalkeeper.

"Here they are!" announced Chalky, walking over to join the team.

Edwin looked towards the German lines and saw the Germans approaching, led by a smartly dressed officer. Behind him came eleven Germans, wearing what looked like proper football shirts, with red and black squares on them. It was only as they drew nearer that Edwin realized the Germans must have spent the night altering and patching those shirts.

Behind the team came the rest of the Germans, wearing greatcoats to keep out the cold.

Lieutenant Pennant stepped forward to greet the Germans, saluting as they arrived. The German officer returned his salute.

"*Guten tag!*" he said. "I am Oberleutnant Felder. Whom do I have the honour of addressing?"

"I am Lieutenant Pennant," said Pennant stiffly. "I am in command here."

"Are your men ready?"

Pennant gestured towards the eleven footballers standing waiting, and the crowd of British soldiers gathered in support.

"As you can see," said Pennant. "We have also made a ball."

And he pointed to a ball that Haddock was holding, which Haddock had made the night before from old rags and scraps of cloth.

"There is no need for that," said the Oberleutnant dismissively, and he gestured at one of his team, who stepped forward, and Edwin saw that he was holding a football, a proper full-sized leather football.

"Who brings a football with them to war?" Chalky muttered to Edwin, bewildered.

Haddock looked down at the ball he had made with such care the night before, spending hours on its construction, and scowled, and threw it to one of his mates.

"Now, the goalposts?" queried Felder.

"We decided to wait and see if you would actually turn up," said Pennant.

Felder bristled.

"We Germans always 'turn up'," he snapped. "I suggest we both build a goal, one at each end."

"Agreed," said Pennant. "We have already marked out the pitch, as you will see, so your men will spot where the goal goes. And we have put posts already in place."

Pennant turned to the soldiers and said: "Harris! Lewis! Whitcombe! Daniels! Put up one goal!"

"Sir!" barked Harris. Then he and three others picked up heavy hammers and headed towards one end of the roughly marked pitch, while four German soldiers made for the other end to erect their goal.

"Now, for referee," said Felder crisply. "I shall be referee."

"No," said Pennant, shaking his head. "You have provided the ball, we shall provide the referee."

"*Nein*," said Felder firmly.

"You think I would not play fair?" demanded Pennant.

Felder hesitated, then he responded: "It is not a question of honour, it is a situation of rank. I am an Oberleutnant, while you are just a Lieutenant. I outrank you."

"I don't think so," disagreed Pennant calmly. "I am a Lieutenant First Class, which is the same rank as an Oberleutnant, I believe. I just did not wish to brag. It is not the British way."

Felder glared at Pennant, then reached into his tunic pocket and produced a whistle.

"But I have a whistle!" he announced.

In answer Pennant produced his own whistle.

"As I have," he replied.

It was Haddock who supplied the answer, and just in time, because Edwin noticed that the players on both sides were getting irritable, mainly through standing around in the cold as they waited, while most of the supporters, well wrapped up in greatcoats, seemed to be enjoying the exchange between the two officers.

"With respect, sir, can't you toss for it?" he appealed to Pennant.

Pennant looked at Felder.

"That seems a sensible suggestion," he said. "Do you agree?"

"I agree," nodded Felder.

Pennent produced a coin, and let Felder choose; to which the German called "heads".

Pennant tossed the coin and let it fall to the ground.

It was "tails".

"Round one to us," whispered Ivor to Edwin.

"I don't think so," whispered back Edwin. "The Lieutenant's very fair-minded. He's more likely to give a decision to the Germans rather than be thought to be cheating."

After the long discussion over the refereeing, the rest of the organization of the match was soon wrapped up. Two linesman were supplied, one from each side; and by this time both goals had been erected.

"At last!" said Ivor, wearily. "I never thought we'd actually get started!"

The two teams took their places on the pitch. Edwin was playing at right half, with Dinny Morris at centre half and Albert Oliver at left half; Jim Haddock and Edgar Field were the two backs; and the forward line read: Bill Kidman, outside right, Jack Lee at outside left; with Ivor Evans inside right, Ewan Mars inside left, and Henry Butt at centre forward.

Pennant strode onto the pitch and brought the two captains forward to toss the coin to decide who would kick off. The Germans won the toss and took their positions. Lieutenant Pennant put his whistle to his lips and blew. The match had begun!

Edwin had played kickabout football in the street with his pals back home in Walsall, and at school, where sometimes he had even been picked for the school team, but nothing like this. Most of the Germans were large muscular men who looked as if they kept themselves fit.Their centre forward was a small thin man, but he made up for his lack of size with dazzling ball control and skill. Twice, early in the game, Edwin tried to stop the German centre forward as he came running at him, but each time he went past Edwin like a will-o'-the-wisp, feinting one way and then the other. Fortunately for Edwin, on both occasions Jim Haddock stepped in and knocked the small German to the ground with a crunching tackle. Unfortunately for Edwin and his team-mates, the second time Haddock did this, Pennant agreed with the boos and shouts of disapproval from the watching Germans, and blew for a foul. The resulting free kick from the German centre half was a ball that curved wickedly after it left his boot, and sailed past big Percy Smith.

As Pennant blew his whistle and pointed to the centre spot, Henry Butt came over to Edwin and muttered, "That German centre forward's a professional, I bet you! No one can bend a ball in the air like that unless they play football professionally. I tell you, Edwin, we're going to have our work cut out against this lot!"

Butt was proved right. During the first half most of the attack and chances fell to the German team, with the British defenders forced to scramble the ball away. By the time the whistle blew for half-time, Edwin felt that they were lucky to be just one goal down.

Jim Haddock did his best at half-time to give an inspirational captain's talk to the rest of the team; but most of them were aware that the Germans were fitter, and also more skilled.

"It's a con," growled Bill Kidman, and he echoed Henry Butt's fears as he added: "I bet you most of this team are professional footballers back home in Germany!"

"That may well be true," admitted Haddock. "But we've got British grit on our side!"

"I'd rather have their centre forward," said Albert Oliver ruefully. Then he looked apologetically at Henry Butt. "No offence, Henry."

"None taken," said Henry graciously. "He's good. Really good."

"Pity no one shot him before the match," muttered Dinny.

The half-time break seemed to end very quickly for Edwin; and then he and the rest of the team were back on the pitch. This time, Henry Butt kicked off, and the British team launched an attack, but it was soon snuffed out by the well-drilled German defence, and once more the ball was passed to the small German centre forward, who came racing towards Edwin. Once again, the German swayed to the left before switching his move to the right; but this time Edwin was ready for him. Edwin stuck out his foot, and the ball bounced up, hit the German, and deflected out to Ivor Evans, who collected it and began to run, shouting and gesturing at Edwin to run towards the German goal.

Henry Butt had already started his own run towards the German goal, and when Ivor passed it towards Edwin, Edwin let it run past him to where Henry could collect it.

Edwin was still running. The two big German backs closed in on Henry, and as they did so he slipped the ball between them, straight to Edwin's feet.

Edwin didn't even look up as the ball came to him, he was aware of the German goalkeeper running towards him, arms outstretched, but then Edwin struck the ball as hard as he could to the goalkeeper's left. The ball went under the goalie's outstretched left arm, hit the inside of the goalpost, and bounced in the goal.

"GOAL!!!"

The shout erupted from the watching British soldiers, and they began jumping up and down, yelling and waving their arms in the air.

Henry and Ivor, the two nearest British players, came to Edwin and slapped him heartily on the back.

"Great goal, boyo!" beamed Ivor.

As Edwin ran back to his position, and the two teams lined up again for the kick-off, Haddock gave Edwin a thumbs up.

"Great stuff, Edwin!" he shouted. "One-all! Now let's go on and win this!"

Edwin's goal seemed to fill both teams with a new sense of purpose: the British delighted that they had put a goal past the seemingly invincible Germans; and the Germans determined to avenge the goal and regain their advantage. As the match restarted, the roars of support from the British soldiers grew louder, as did the chants from the German spectators. And then the singing started, not Christmas carols this time, but national anthems.

The Germans began first with fiery choruses of "*Deutschland Über Alles*", and as soon as the British soldiers realized what was happening, they retaliated with loud and repeated renditions of "God Save Our Gracious King".

Meanwhile, on the pitch the game became a series of fierce attacks against stubborn defences, first at the British end, and then at the German end, with play see-sawing as the ball went from player to player, was snatched off them, and then booted up the pitch to the other end. And then, just as it looked as if the game was going to end as a draw, a loose ball in the centre of the pitch was gathered up by the small German centre forward; but this time, instead of going off on one of his darting dazzling runs, he hoofed the ball high into the air.

In the British goal, Percy Smith looked up, searching for the ball in the sky, but the winter sun had chosen that moment to come out, and Percy found himself looking directly into it, dazzled. He put his hand above his eyes to try and cut out the sun, but…

"GOAL!!!"

This time it was the Germans who were leaping about, shouting and roaring and waving their arms in delight.

The ball had come down right beside Percy, and bounced in between the goalposts while Percy was still trying to focus in the blinding glare of the sun.

There was not even time to restart the game. Lieutenant Pennant blew for the goal, looked at his watch, and then blew again for the final whistle.

Haddock glared towards the Lieutenant as Pennant walked off the pitch towards the German Oberleutnant to shake hands.

"Pennant blew too early," he complained bitterly to Edwin. "He should have given us more time. And that was a cheat of a goal. Kicking it up in the air so that poor old Percy was blinded by the sun!"

"They were good, though," said Edwin.

"They had luck on their side," retorted Haddock grumpily.

"And that little centre forward," said Ivor. "I wonder who he is?"

"His name's Beckenbauer," said Henry Butt, joining them. "I asked one of the Germans."

"Huh!" snorted Haddock. "Germans! What do they know about football?"

25 December 1914–24 April 1915

It was on Christmas Day, 1914, at Frelinghien in France, on the Western Front, a place where the enemy troops faced each other across barbed wire, that soldiers from both sides came out of their trenches and a rough pitch was marked out in No Man's Land; and a team from the 1st Battalion, the Royal Welch Fusiliers, played a football game against a team made up of German soldiers from Battalion 371.

There are different versions of the score, with some reports saying that the Germans won 2-1, while others say the score was 3-2 to the Germans. What is generally agreed and accepted was that the game was a victory for the German side.

This was not the only example of a Christmas truce in 1914: along the front line it has been estimated that as many as 100,000 British and German soldiers were involved in unofficial truces. These included meetings and exchanges of gifts. Captain Bruce Bairnsfather from the Royal Warwickshire Regiment, who served throughout the First World War, recalled the unofficial truce: "I spotted a German officer, some sort of lieutenant, and being a bit of a collector, I intimated to him that I had taken a fancy to some of his buttons. I brought out my wire clippers and with a few deft snips removed a couple of his buttons and put them in my pocket. I then gave him two of mine in exchange. The last thing I saw was one of my machine gunners, who was a bit of an amateur hairdresser in civilian life, cutting the unnaturally long hair of a Boche, who was patiently kneeling on the ground whilst the hair clippers went to work on his neck."

Not everyone approved of these unofficial truces. Allied commanders issued firm orders that there should be no further such fraternization between British and enemy troops; and a young Austrian soldier called Adolf Hitler, serving in the trenches with the Bavarian Reserve Infantry Regiment, was furious, accusing the German soldiers who took part in these "truces" of being unmilitary in their conduct: "Such things should not happen in wartime. Have you Germans no sense of honour at all?"

But, as we have seen, the War was not confined to the Western Front of the trenches of France, nor just to Britain and the other countries of Europe. This was a *World* War.

On 14 January 1915, South African forces occupied Swakopmund in South-West Africa; and four days later, on 18 January 1915, the Germans were victorious at Jassin in East Africa.

In the Far East, on 18 January 1915, Japan used its alliance with Britain to present its old enemy, China, with a list of demands that, if not met, Japan said would constitute an act of war. China at that time was struggling with internal problems, and so acceded to Japan's demands, rather than be involved in a full-scale war. However, Britain interceded to stop one of Japan's demands, which was that China should accept Japanese "advisers" at every level of Chinese Government, Japan's way of trying to rule China by stealth.

In the Middle East, Turkey was seen by both sides as key to the Arab world. In the early months of the War, Britain tried to forge an alliance with Turkey; unaware that the Turkish Government had already signed a secret defensive alliance with the Germans on 14 July 1914.

This alliance was the result of heavy German investment in Turkey during the winter period of 1913–1914, when Germany built the Berlin-Baghdad railway, as well as forging important links in banking, trade and military affairs with the Turks. The Allies only really became aware of Turkey's military affiliation with Germany on 29 October 1914, when the Germans launched an attack on Russian Army bases in the Black Sea from a Turkish base, with the full co-operation of the Turks. As a result, on 5 November 1914, Britain declared war on Turkey.

One of the biggest areas of concern to the Allies, once they realized that Turkey had sided with Germany, was the Dardanelles Straits. The Dardanelles Straits was the key link between Russia's Black Sea ports and the Mediterranean. The Straits are about 65 km long, and only 7 km wide at their widest point, with some stretches only 1,600 metres wide. The Straits are known for their difficult currents. On the north-western shore they are overlooked by the high cliffs of the Gallipoli Peninsula. With the Straits in Turkish hands, a vital supply route between Russia and the Mediterranean would be cut.

In February and March 1915, there was an attempt by Anglo-French warships to try to force a passage through the Turkish-held Dardanelles

Straits. The attempt failed. The Turkish forces, backed up by German troops and commanders, were in secure positions on land which the British and French found impossible to dislodge from the sea.

It was now that Britain called on its colonies, Australia and New Zealand, to send fighting forces to try to dislodge the Turkish defences. The Anzacs (the Australian and New Zealand Army Corps) answered that call.

Anzac Cove

25 April 1915

"Aaaaargh!" Wiz Wilson crumpled to the beach with a howl of agony.

Danny Murphy dropped his end of the empty stretcher and started to move towards the fallen Wiz. When bullets began to smack into the ground around him, he threw himself down behind a rock, and muttered a silent prayer of thanks for the rocks and boulders strewn around the beach.

The firing moved away from him, and Danny crawled towards Wiz.

"Where are you hit?" he asked.

"Me leg!" moaned Wiz.

The bullet looked like it was still inside Wiz's leg; there was no exit wound, just blood spreading and soaking on the front of Wiz's trousers.

Quickly, Danny ripped the trousers open to expose the wound, and as he did so, Wiz screamed again, and Danny realized that the bullet had broken Wiz's leg. The wound was pumping blood; the artery had been hit. As gently as he could, Danny put a tourniquet around Wiz's leg and tightened it, stopping the blood pumping. Then he pulled two splints from the stretcher end and began to bind Wiz's leg with them, keeping the break from worsening.

"Trouble, mate?"

Danny turned, and then stopped, stunned. There was another medical orderly standing there, identified by his Red-Cross armband, but he was holding a length of rope – and at the end of the rope was a donkey.

The man looked at Wiz's leg approvingly.

"Good job," he nodded.

"Yes, but I can't get him to the shore," said Danny. He gestured to the stretcher, lying on the shingle.

The man grinned.

"No problem," he said. "That's where Duffy comes in!"

With that, the man bent down and hauled Wiz up. Wiz moaned in pain, but held onto the man's shoulders as he lifted Wiz onto the back of the donkey.

"There!" he said.

"So you're Duffy," said Danny.

The man laughed.

"No!" he chuckled. "Duffy's the donkey. My name's Simpson. John Simpson."

"I'm Danny Murphy," said Danny. "This here's Wiz."

"Well, we'd better get Wiz to the boats," said Simpson.

Suddenly the firing from the Turkish troops high up on the cliffs returned to where they stood, and bullets smacked into the sand and shingle around them, narrowly missing them.

"Better move before they get their aim on us," said Simpson. "Let's hope they won't shoot at a donkey!"

With that, Simpson gave a tug at the rope and the donkey moved forward, Wiz on its back, clinging to its mane. Danny followed, carrying the rolled-up stretcher and medical bag.

As if by a miracle, the shooting moved away from them and began to be directed at troops in the trenches that had been dug along the beach, with low walls of sand and shingle piled up in front.

Danny, Simpson and the donkey made their way across the beach towards the water's edge, where small boats waited to ferry the wounded out to the larger troop ships moored offshore.

Danny and the rest of the troops had been trapped on this beach ever since thousands of them had been landed by the small open invasion boats at dawn the day before. The open boats had been towed by tugs, ferrying them across from the larger Royal Navy boats that had brought them all the way from Egypt. On the long journey to Gallipoli they'd been told that the Turkish positions had been softened up by shelling from British and French naval ships, that the Turkish defences would collapse when this massive invasion force of nearly half a million soldiers – a combined attack force from Britain, France, India, and Australia and New Zealand – landed and began to advance inland.

The reality was very different. Most of the Turkish positions were on high ground overlooking the beaches. There were some lower down, across scrubland, but these were heavily protected by barbed wire and machine guns, as well as the machine guns on the higher ground. The hills behind the beach were carved through with ravines and gullies, overgrown with scrub, trees and bushes, and also protected by rolls and rolls of barbed wire.

The first wave of troops landing on the beaches and advancing forward had been cut down by machine-gun and rifle fire. Some made it to the barbed wire, but found themselves tangled up in it, strung up on the wire, easy targets.

Once the landing invasion had begun, the shelling of the Turkish positions by the big navy ships offshore had been halted for fear of shells hitting the Allied troops. As a result, the troops had found themselves pinned down. They were unable to move forward. With the sea behind them, they couldn't retreat. All they could do was dig trenches as best they could to give them some kind of cover against the Turkish fire, while their officers drew up plans for a major assault on the Turkish lines. And the longer it took for that assault to take place, the more troops joined those already dug in on the beach as the invasion craft brought more soldiers out from the anchored ships. As a result, this beach, and the others along the coast, were a mass of thousands of men, trapped, doing their best to fire back, and stay alive.

Danny and Wiz were part of 3rd Field Ambulance, Australian Army Medical Corps, as was the bloke with the donkey, John Simpson. Danny hadn't spoken to Simpson before, but that wasn't unusual, the troopships bringing them all here from Australia had been packed. And not just with Aussies, there seemed to be just as many Kiwis from New Zealand. As Wiz had said when they'd seen the huge numbers of men boarding the ships at the port in Egypt: "Strewth, our countries are going to be empty!"

Danny and Simpson reached the shore and they waded out in the sea up to their knees, to the nearest waiting boat. There, they lifted Wiz off the back of the donkey and handed him to the waiting sailors, who laid him down between the rows of seats. There were other wounded men already in the boat, bandaged and patched up.

"Sorry I've got to leave you like this, Danny!" said Wiz, forcing out the words through teeth clenched against the pain.

"No worries," said Danny. He gestured back towards the beach, where the firing continued. "I don't think we'll be going anywhere else any time soon."

"OK!" called the sailor in charge. "We've got enough to make the journey worthwhile."

Four sailors jumped out of the boat and began to push it into the waves, off the shingle that held it, out into deeper water, and soon it was afloat and moving away from the shore, long oars at the side of the boat pushing it out to sea, taking it out to the nearest tugboat, which would take it to the mother ships.

"Right," said Simpson. He looked up. "That sun in the sky tells me it's time for the old nosebag to go on." He gestured towards one of the trenches and Danny saw smoke rising from it. "And it looks to me like someone's got a stewpot going! We're in the right place, right time! Come on! Tucker time!" He led the donkey back out of the water and helped Danny fix the stretcher and medical bag on the donkey's back. Then they headed towards the nearby trench. As Simpson had spotted, someone had got a stewpot cooking, a broth of some kind, which they were happy to share with Danny and Simpson. Simpson seemed to be a familiar figure here, because the men joked with him about the donkey, most of them suggesting different names for it, many of them coming up with rude suggestions, or suggesting it be named after some of their generals. To all of them, Simpson shook his head. "This donkey's called Duffy. That's the name he likes best, so that's who he is."

As Danny and Simpson sat, supping their stew, Danny asked the question that had been in his mind ever since he'd first encountered Simpson shortly before.

"Where's he from? You didn't bring him with you?"

Simpson laughed.

"Don't be stupid! You think they'd have let me bring a donkey on a troopship?" He reached out and patted the animal affectionately. "I found him."

"Found him? Where?"

"Here. On the beach, yesterday, when we landed."

"But ... where did he come from?"

"Who knows?" shrugged Simpson. "My guess is he wandered here from somewhere, and once the shooting started he decided to stay. Me and Duffy have been moving blokes off the beach ever since. Haven't you seen us?"

"To be honest, I've spent most of the time watching out for the Turks shooting at us," admitted Danny. "Someone said there was a bloke with a donkey here, but I didn't believe it. Until now." He looked at Duffy, then at Simpson. "How did you get him to carry Wiz, with all this firing going on?"

"Donkeys trust me," replied Simpson. "I was brought up with 'em. When I was a nipper in South Shields I used to help run the donkeys on the beach."

"Where's South Shields?" asked Danny.

"North-East England," said Simpson.

"So you're a Pom," said Danny.

Simpson shook his head.

"Not any more. I've been in Oz long enough for it to be my home."

"Whereabouts?"

"All over. I did cane-cutting and worked on a station in Queensland. I was a coalminer at Coledale; then at Corrimal and Mount Kembla. I was in the Yilgarn goldfield in Western Australia. For the past couple of years, before I joined up with this lot, I've been working the boats around the coast. Steward, fireman and greaser, that's me."

"You don't look much older than me, but you've seen more of Australia than I have in my whole life," admitted Danny.

"I'm twenty-two," said Simpson. "You?"

"Nineteen. And before this, I'd never been further than Melbourne."

"Well you've made up for it now," said Simpson. "Halfway around the world to get here."

"My dad didn't want me to join up," said Danny. "He was angry with me."

"Oh? Why?"

Danny hesitated, then said: "My family are Irish originally."

Simpson laughed.

"No!" he said in mock disbelief. "With a name like Murphy! Who'd have thought it!"

"Yeah, well," continued Danny awkwardly. "My dad don't like the English. He reckons they've been killing our people for centuries. The famine. Oliver Cromwell. And even now he says they keep the Irish as slaves and won't give us a free country."

"You've got a free country," said Simpson. "You're an Australian."

"It's still part of the Empire, though, and my dad says that the Irish should fight against the Brits, not for them."

"What, with the Germans and the Turks?"

Danny looked uncomfortable.

"No," he said. "He doesn't go that far. But he doesn't feel that those of us who are Irish should be fighting for the Brits. He says it's betraying all the people who've gone before, who died fighting for Ireland."

"And what do you feel?" asked Simpson.

Danny hesitated, then he said: "I think we have to stick together. I've got cousins in England as well as Ireland, and I think it's like we're all family."

Simpson nodded.

"I think you're right," he said. "If you ask me, sooner or later you've got to look at the picture, and say: Who's on my side *now*? Not a hundred years ago. Or two hundred years. I mean, not so long ago the English and the French were at war. Now, here they are, fighting side by side." He looked thoughtful. "Most of all, it's being on the side that's right."

"But who is?" asked Danny helplessly. "To be honest, I'm not even sure what this war is all about. I just know that when my mates joined up, I couldn't let them down. I had to go with them."

A voice interrupted them – a soldier running up and calling down to them in the trench.

"Medics!" he panted. "Two of my mates are down!"

Immediately Simpson emptied the remains of his stew from his billycan and stood up.

"We're with you!" he said. "Come on, Danny!"

Danny climbed out of the trench and followed Simpson as he grabbed the end of Duffy's rope and set off after the soldier.

Two men were lying on the shingle behind some scrub where their mates had dragged them. The scrub didn't afford much protection, but it shielded the men from the Turks' gunsights. One of the soldiers was unconscious, one leg twisted crookedly, and one of his arms also obviously broken, the bone protruding out from his sleeve just below the elbow. The other was conscious and moaning in pain.

"Digger took it in both legs," said the soldier who'd called them. He looked at the unconscious soldier with the broken arm and leg. "Josh got hit everywhere. Legs and arms." He looked worried. "I think he might be dead."

Simpson knelt down next to the unconscious man and felt for his pulse.

"No," he said. "He's alive, just." He looked at Danny. "You see what you can do with Digger, I'll see if I can patch the other one up enough to get them to the boats. One on the stretcher, one on the donkey. Right, Danny?"

"Right," nodded Danny.

Danny took out his scissors and cut away Digger's leggings around the bullet wounds, while Simpson set to work on the unconscious Josh.

"It doesn't look like the bones are broken," said Danny. "But your muscles are torn apart."

"Will I walk again?" asked Digger, his face creased with pain.

"I don't see why not," said Danny. "But not soon."

"OK, I'm ready here," said Simpson, standing up. "Danny?"

"Ready," said Danny. He gestured at Digger. "I think he's the one for the donkey."

"I was thinking the same," agreed Simpson.

Together, Simpson and Danny lifted Digger off the ground and laid him over Duffy's back. Then they put the still unconscious Josh on the stretcher. Simpson took the end of Duffy's halter rope in his hand, then managed to lift his end of the stretcher, as Danny lifted the other end.

"OK," he said. "Let's go!"

As they set off for the shore, leaving the cover of the shrub, the firing from the Turkish positions opened up on them, bullets slamming into the sand and shingle by their feet.

"Can't they see the red cross on our sleeves?" said Danny angrily, as he moved forward, holding the weight of the stretcher.

"Not from that distance," said Simpson.

With Danny at the front and Simpson with Duffy following behind, they made it across the open beach, bullets smashing around them.

"Not very good shots, are they?" said Simpson. "I mean, you'd have thought we'd be an easy target: two men with a stretcher and a donkey."

They reached the shore, but this time there were no boats waiting for them; they were all out at sea, either heading out to the steamboat tugs, or coming back towards shore. Danny looked along the shoreline and saw that there were so many wounded, they were being left by the water's edge to wait for the next boat to come and pick them up, some of them sitting up, while others were laid out in rows. *Like corpses*, thought Danny. But the dead didn't get the dignity of being evacuated, they lay where they fell. He'd seen them, the bodies lying on the beach. Now and then their mates tried to pull the bodies of their dead comrades back into cover, but the Turks just shot at them when they tried to do that, resulting in more casualties. And so the dead lay there, exposed, a grim reminder of the fate that lay in store for every man on that beach.

As day turned to dusk, the firing from both sides quietened down, and then stopped. Simpson made sure that Duffy the donkey was fed and watered before he settled down with Danny and other members of the Ambulance Unit in one of the trenches. As they ate their evening meal, this one another stew with hard biscuits, talk was all about what the next stage would be.

"I heard they're going to get our blokes to push forward, try and break through their lines and get behind the Turks," said one, Bluey Johnson, as he chewed on his biscuits.

"I heard they're expecting the Turks to launch a counter-attack," put in another, Mick Harrigan.

"Typical!" sighed Simpson. "Rumour and more rumour. It's often struck me the people at the top treat us ordinary blokes like mushrooms."

"Mushrooms?" said Danny.

"Yeah," nodded Simpson. "We're kept in the dark and fed a load of manure."

The others laughed.

"Well I can tell you one thing I know for sure," said Lofty Green, a very tall thin medico. "The engineers are going to start putting up a field hospital at each end of the beach. I heard it from one of the engineers himself."

"A field hospital," mused Bluey thoughtfully. "Sounds like they think we're going to be here for a while, mates."

Next morning, Danny and Simpson went to check that Duffy was all right, then took him with them when they joined their unit to wait for the action to begin. In the trenches dug along the beach, the soldiers settled themselves down behind their sandy protective ridges and waited for orders.

Today, there was little firing from the Turkish positions, just an occasional patch of sporadic shooting, and then silence.

"Something's happening," Simpson murmured to Danny. "The calm before the storm."

"Think there's gonna be an attack?" asked Danny.

"Yes," said Simpson. "But not from our side. If there was, orders would have been issued already. But the fact the Turks aren't shooting means they're getting ready." He looked thoughtful, and then called out: "Any of you lads fancy a bet!"

"What sort of bet?" asked Lofty.

"Ten to one the Turks launch an attack."

"That's no bet," said Mick, shaking his head. "I told you, that's what I heard yesterday, and someone's got that information from somewhere. I reckon someone's been watching the Turks up close and reporting back."

"OK," said Simpson. "How long before they attack? I say it'll be before noon."

Bluey looked at his watch.

"It's half past ten now," he said. "That only gives them an hour and a half. I'll take that bet."

"A pound," said Simpson, putting out his hand to shake on the deal.

Bluey shook his head.

"Too rich for me!" he said. "A shilling."

"A shilling?" echoed Simpson scornfully. "What sort of bet is that?"

"One I can afford to pay if you win."

"Look, if the Turks attack it's likely that some of us will be killed, so we'll never get to collect the winnings anyway," said Simpson.

"That's a cheerful way of looking at it!" complained Mick.

Bluey shook his head.

"A shilling if the Turks attack before noon," he said. "If they attack after noon, you lose and you pay me a shilling."

"Done," said Simpson.

The two men shook hands, and settled down with the rest to scan the Turkish positions. There seemed to be no sign of any activity on the top of the hills, or in the valleys.

"Maybe they've packed up and left," said Danny hopefully.

"Not a chance," said Simpson. "Believe me, they're going to attack. I can sense it." He looked at his watch. "I hope they do it soon. It's ten to twelve."

They continued scanning the skyline and the entrances to the ravines and valleys that led from the beach to the hills. The soldiers in the trenches had also picked up the expectation that an attack was imminent, because all along the beach Danny could see rifles being made ready and ammunition being prepared, and machine-gun posts manned.

Simpson got out of the trench and went to where Duffy was grazing on a piece of scrub poking through the shingle, and led the donkey down into the trench.

"You can't bring an animal down here!" protested Mick.

"Duffy is one of us and more useful than some," said Simpson. "I'm not taking any chances on some Turk shooting him."

Suddenly they heard the shrill sound of a whistle from a nearby trench – then another.

"They're coming!" shouted Mick.

Both Simpson and Bluey looked at their watches.

"Quarter past twelve!" crowed Bluey, and he gave a triumphant chuckle, and then made a choking sound and crumpled to the trench in a heap, blood pumping from the back of his head.

Immediately, the others dived down and crawled away as gunfire raked the top of their trench, bullets ricocheting.

From the other trenches came the sound of rifle and machine-gun fire.

Danny pulled himself up to the top of the trench and peered through a gap in the ridge of stones and sand. The Turks had appeared from the mouths of the valleys, masses of them, running towards the Anzac lines, rifles levelled and firing. More were coming out from the ravines and gullies further along the beach. They had obviously been making their way down from their hillside positions, using the trees and bushes and gullies to conceal their advance, but now they were out in the open, thousands of them, a moving wall of men and rifles launched in what looked to be a suicidal attack against the Anzac trenches. As the front line of Turks fell to the Anzac defensive fire, more came, and kept coming, thousands of them. Danny had heard that the Turks had one of the largest armies in this war, but the size of the force coming at them stunned him. Surely the Anzac trenches would be overwhelmed! But the soldiers in the trenches kept up their fire, accurate and deadly. The machine-gun posts added to it, their fire raking the Turkish lines with murderous effect. Now the

Turks were advancing over the bodies of their dead, but still they came on, still firing. Bullets zinged past Danny and ploughed into the trench's rear wall and the defensive ridge of sand and shingle in front of the trench. Closer and closer they came, and now Danny could see their faces. Young men, just like him, advancing, being shot, crumpling to the ground, with more coming on.

Suddenly, above the ear-splitting noise of gunfire that echoed over his head and around him, he heard the sound of a whistle in the distance, a long, shrill sound that was suddenly cut off, and then began again, a mournful high-pitched keening whistle.

This time, the troops at the front of the Turkish advance stopped, and then began to retreat, walking backwards, still firing their rifles. The soldiers in the Anzac trenches continued shooting, and Danny saw more Turks tumble to the ground before the signal was given in the trenches to cease fire. But the Anzac soldiers kept their rifles poised and ready, in case it was merely a ploy and the Turks attacked again.

They didn't. The Turks withdrew back into the ravines and gullies, and then disappeared.

Danny looked out at the scene of devastation before him. Literally thousands of dead Turkish soldiers lay on the beach. He was sure he saw movements out there among the rows of bodies, some Turks who had been badly wounded, and were now dying.

"Someone should help them," he said, gesturing towards the killing ground.

"That's up to the Turks," said Mick. "We've got our own to look after."

And he stepped over Bluey's dead body and began to climb out of the trench.

Simpson looked down at the body and gave a sigh.

"He should have bet a pound," he said sadly.

Then he took hold of Duffy's rope and led him towards the ramp out of the trench. After a moment, Danny followed.

27 April 1915–10 October 1915

John Simpson Kirkpatrick called himself just "John Simpson" when he signed up with the Australian and New Zealand Army Corps as a stretcher bearer. One suggestion has been made that he did this to avoid being identified as the same John Simpson Kirkpatrick who'd deserted from the merchant navy soon after arriving in Australia. Known as "the man with the donkey" because of his work carrying injured soldiers to safety with the aid of a donkey he found on the beach at Gallipoli, Simpson Kirkpatrick was shot and killed by Turkish rifle fire on 19 May 1915, just three and a half weeks after the landings. After Kirkpatrick's death, Duffy the donkey was taken over by Dick Henderson, a stretcher bearer with the New Zealand Medical Corps, who carried on using the donkey to rescue wounded soldiers. In later years, Henderson said the donkey's name was actually Murphy.

The Gallipoli campaign saw massive loss of life on both sides, but with no military advantage to the Allies. The campaign had begun early in 1915, with attacks on the Turkish positions on the Gallipoli Peninsula by ships of the British and French navies, but these attempted assaults had failed, or been aborted. On 25 April 1915, the first proper assaults by ground forces were launched with the landing of Australian and New Zealand troops at Anzac Cove, and British and French troops at Cape Helles on the Gallipoli Peninsula. They met fierce resistance from the Turkish forces, and for the next few months there was stalemate as the Allies tried to advance, and the Turkish defended, with no ground gained by either side.

Finally, by the end of 1915, it was accepted that the Gallipoli campaign had failed. The Anzac forces were withdrawn during December 1915, with the final British troops being evacuated on 9 January 1916.

In total 480,000 Allied troops took part in the campaign – from Britain, France, Australia, New Zealand, Senegal, India, Newfoundland, Russia, and the Syrian Jewish community. The Allies suffered 43 per cent casualties (205,000 dead or wounded); 43,000 British and British Empire soldiers died (including 1,370 Indians), as well as 15,000 French. However, it was not just the battle action that caused the deaths. The conditions at Gallipoli were terrible, leading to disease and sickness to such a degree that it was calculated that 145,000 of the Allied casualties were due to dysentery, diarrhoea and enteric fever caught as a result of the appalling conditions: flies and vermin thriving on the bodies of the dead.

The Anzac troops bore the brunt of the casualties, with 33,600, including 8,700 Australians and 2,700 New Zealanders dead. The casualty figures may appear smaller than those of the British and French forces, but when those deaths are taken as a percentage of the population of the countries at that time, Australia and New Zealand suffered a massive percentage loss.

The actual number of Turkish deaths has never been officially published, but estimates put them at around 250,000.

There was a rare and poignant postscript to the Dardanelles campaign: The commander of the Turkish forces at Anzac Cove was Mustafa Kemal Atatürk, who became founder and first President of the Turkish Republic in 1923. In 1934, Atatürk published a tribute in memory of the Anzac forces:

THE ANZAC MEMORIAL
Those heroes that shed their blood and lost their lives
You are now lying in the soil of a friendly country.
Therefore, rest in peace.
There is no difference between the Johnnies
And the Mehmets to us where they lie side by side
Here in this country of ours.
You, the mothers who sent their sons from far away countries
Wipe away your tears.
Your sons are now lying in our bosom and are in peace.
After having lost their lives on this land, they have
Become our sons as well.

Meanwhile, on other fighting fronts, and on the seas and oceans of the world, the War continued.

On 7 May 1915, the passenger liner *Lusitania* was torpedoed by German U-boats off the coast of Ireland, near Kinsale, County Cork.

The *Lusitania* had been sailing from New York to Britain with 1,900 passengers and crew on board, and 1,198 people died in this attack, including 124 American citizens. Although the German Government apologized for the attack, claiming the *Lusitania* had been attacked by mistake, the sinking of the civilian passenger ship provoked outrage, and caused many Americans to question the neutral position of the United States in the War.

Later that same month, on 31 May, a German Zeppelin – a huge gas-filled airship – dropped bombs on London. There had been Zeppelin attacks on Britain before, but this was the first time that Britain's capital city had been bombed.

In Europe, away from the Western Front in France, Austria-Germany moved into Poland during the summer of 1915. Poland was a divided country: part of it was a province of Imperial Russia, while Austria-Hungary and Germany claimed other parts. From June 1915, most of Poland came under German rule.

Also in June, Austria-Germany launched a series of offensives against Italy. For many years, Italy and Austria-Germany had been in dispute about the ownership of the lands along their borders. Also, Italy had made an agreement with Britain with the Treaty of London in 1915 to take military action against Germany. However, Italy was recovering from a debilitating war with Turkey (1911–1912) and was short of military supplies. The attack on Italy by Austria-Germany was to lead to another stalemate, as casualties mounted, but neither side gained any advantage. Despite its weakened military situation, on

20 August, as part of its commitment to the Allied cause, Italy declared war on Turkey.

The War was also being fought in the Middle East. Fighting in Turkish Mesopotamia (later part of Persia, and now called Iraq) had begun in November 1914, with a combined Indian-Anglo force sent to protect vital oil supplies from the enemy. This developed into a full-scale war between Allied (mainly Indian and British) and Turkish forces. At first, the Allied forces were short of arms and ammunition, as well as troops, because most of the Allies' resources were still being poured into the Western Front, but in September 1915 the Allies had a major victory in Mesopotamia at Es Sinn, when an advance by the Indian 6th Division forced the Turks to retreat back to within 49 km of Baghdad.

On the Western Front, in the trenches of France, 1915 had been a year of carnage and stalemate.

In April, at Ypres, the Germans used poison gas for the first time, sending chlorine gas towards the French positions. The French troops, completely unprepared and unprotected against the gas, retreated, leaving a gap 5 miles wide in the front line. This exposed the Canadian forces, who occupied the next position on the front line. However, the Germans weren't prepared to go into clouds of their own poison gas, and held back from advancing. The Canadians then moved to fill the positions vacated by the French. To counter the gas, the Canadians used handkerchiefs, towels and bandages soaked in urine as improvised respirators. This brave action meant they were in position to stop the Germans from advancing when the gas cleared.

In May, British and Indian troops advanced 1,000 metres at Neuve Chapelle, but then were forced to stop. This battle resulted in 13,000 Allied losses, and 12,000 Germans.

The casualty rates mounted: at Artois, in five weeks of fighting the French suffered 100,000 casualties and the Germans 60,000. At Festubert, the British suffered 16,000 casualties in the twelve-day period between 15 and 27 May.

As the death toll increased, there was little gain of territory by either side. The Allies might gain a couple of hundred metres of ground, but then they would be pushed back the same distance over the next few weeks. Then the Germans would force an advance and gain a few hundred metres before they, in turn, were pushed back.

In September 1915, the French, along with their Moroccan Division, launched a major attack against the German lines at Champagne and Artois, advancing nearly 3,000 metres before the attack was stopped by strong German defences. The French suffered losses of 144,000 in this attack, and the Germans 85,000.

On 25 September, Field Marshal Sir Douglas Haig, the British military leader, gave orders for poison gas to be used against the Germans for the first time. The effect was mixed: although it gave the 9th Scottish Division the advantage in their successful attack on the German positions at the previously impregnable Hohenzoller Redoubt and Haisnes, elsewhere the wind blew the poison gas back across the British trenches.

Meanwhile, in Brussels, Belgium, a 49-year-old British nurse, Edith Cavell, was arrested by the German authorities and charged with helping more than 200 Allied soldiers to escape across the border from Belgium into neutral Holland.

Edith Cavell

12 October 1915

Fourteen-year-old Lisette Sim sat at the kitchen table in her family's small house in the back streets of Brussels and watched her father in his armchair doing his best to read the newspaper, but failing. He was worried, as was Lisette. As her father shot another anxious look at the clock, Lisette thought: *He is wondering where Mother is. She is normally home from work by this time.*

Her mother worked as a cleaner at the Town Hall in the centre of Brussels – although it was no longer the Town Hall, it was now the headquarters of the German Army. It was a dangerous place to work. Anywhere in Brussels was a dangerous place since the Germans invaded. The German soldiers strutted around the city, ordering the locals around, intimidating them with their rifles. Lisette wasn't sure whether their aggressive manner was arrogance at having invaded and conquered Belgium, or fear in case the Belgians rose up against them.

Mother will be all right, Lisette did her best to reassure herself, but as the clock ticked further on, the worry over what had happened to her mother made her edgy, too.

Suddenly her father got up, throwing down his newspaper.

"I will go out and find her!" he announced.

He was heading to the door, when there was the sound of the key in the lock, the door opened, and Madame Sim came in.

They could both tell from her expression that something bad had happened. What could it be? *So many things*, thought Lisette. *The German soldiers on the street, acting tough. Or maybe something had happened at German HQ?* Then Lisette thought of the English nurse, Nurse Edith, who had been held prisoner inside the German HQ for the past two months, suspected of spying. Everyone knew the Germans wanted to kill her as an example to stop other people from spying against them.

"What's wrong?" asked Monsieur Sim. "Did the soldiers trouble you on your way home?"

Madame Sim shook her head.

"No," she said. "Something … happened at the Town Hall."

"The Englishwoman?" blurted out Lisette fearfully. "Nurse Edith?"

Madame Sim nodded.

"Yes," she said unhappily.

"What has happened?" demanded Monsieur Sim. "Have they killed her?" He swore angrily. "Those German swine!"

"No," said Madame Sim, shaking her head. "They … they want Lisette to be Nurse Edith's maid while she is in prison."

Lisette and her father stared at one another, stunned, bewildered.

"What?" asked Lisette.

"Why?" asked her father, equally baffled.

Madame Sim sank down onto a chair, her face ashen.

"That is why I was late," she said. "The Commandant, Herzer, sent for me as I was about to leave."

Her face troubled by the memory, she told them of the encounter. Madame Sim hadn't wanted to work for the Germans, but the Resistance had asked her to take the job and try to keep them informed of what was going on inside the building. So far, Madame Sim had been unable to pick up any information that could be used against the Germans. Security was very strict, and Madame Sim wasn't allowed anywhere near where sensitive information was stored, or even discussed. Until today, when she'd been stopped by the Commandant himself as she put on her coat to leave the building.

"Ah, Frau Sim!" Herzer had called.

He was standing in the doorway of his office, hands behind his back as always, his pose stiff and formal, his uniform immaculate, his hair shorn almost to the point of baldness, peering at her through the lenses of his round glasses.

"I wish to have a word with you before you leave! In my office, please."

Madame Sim could feel herself trembling beneath her coat as she entered the Commandant's office. What had happened? Why had he called her? Had he somehow discovered that she had been asked by the Resistance to take the job of cleaner? Was she going to be arrested as a spy? She knew what happened to spies: they were tortured, and then shot.

Herzer followed her into his office and shut the door. He did not invite her to sit down, nor did he sit down behind his desk. Instead, he stood directly in front of her, studying her thoughtfully. Then he said: "You have a daughter, I believe. A fourteen-year-old girl."

"Yes," nodded Madame Sim.

"Her name?" asked Herzer.

Once again, Madame Sim felt herself trembling. Had something terrible happened to Lisette?

"Is she in trouble?" she blurted out, fearfully.

Herzer frowned.

"Not to my knowledge," he said. "In fact, I believe I may have some good news for her. Her name?" he repeated, firmer this time.

"Lisette," said Madame Sim, her voice a whisper.

Herzer nodded.

"And am I correct in thinking that she was once a patient of the English nurse when she was in hospital? By the English nurse, I am referring to the spy, Edith Cavell."

Yes, thought Madame Sim: *Edith Cavell, the English nurse who was currently being held here at German HQ.* She wanted to burst out a challenge and say: "Edith Cavell is not a spy! She is a brave and good woman and a patriot!" But, instead, she said: "Yes, Lisette was in hospital two years ago, when she was twelve years old. She was seriously ill, but Mam'selle Cavell nursed her through her illness, and thankfully, Lisette was returned to us."

Herzer nodded impatiently.

"Yes," he snapped sarcastically. "We have all been told how good this woman was as a nurse." Then he made an effort and controlled his obvious anger, and forced a smile. "In fact, we feel that it is …unfortunate that she is in her current situation."

Her current situation, thought Madame Sim bitterly. Edith Cavell sits in solitary confinement in your dungeons while you try to force her into a confession of treason, or "aiding the enemy". But how can Edith Cavell be guilty of treason when she is British, not German? wondered Madame Sim. But then, the Germans were the victors, they made the rules.

"The point is that we wish to make Fräulein Cavell's situation less inhospitable," continued Herzer. "To that end I have decided to employ a maid for her, to take her meals to her, to collect the empty dishes, and carry out any other duties that Fräulein Cavell wishes. She is familiar with your daughter, and to have a friendly face here might make her situation feel less … oppressive. So, please advise your daughter that her presence is required here from tomorrow morning. You will bring her with you when you report for duty."

Madame Sim stared at the Commandant, her mind in a whirl. No, this was not going to happen! She would not allow her daughter to be dragged into this dreadful place, into this dreadful war!

"I am not sure if Lisette will be able to take on the duties you mention, Herr Commandant—" she began apologetically, but Herzer cut her off, his voice sharp, icy.

"You do not understand," he snapped. "This is not a request. It is an order. Your daughter will report here tomorrow morning and begin her duties as the maid of the Englishwoman."

And with that he had dismissed Madame Sim.

"But … why?" asked Monsieur Sim, bewildered.

"Because he hopes she will talk about her actions to me, and then he will have the evidence he needs to find her guilty," said Lisette miserably.

Everyone in Brussels knew the story. The Englishwoman, Edith Cavell, had been working as a nurse, and teaching others to be nurses at the teaching hospital in Brussels, since 1907. When the Germans invaded Belgium in 1914, Edith had been away in England, visiting her mother. Most locals had expected her to remain in England, but instead Edith had returned to Brussels to continue her nursing and teaching work. It had been an act of brave defiance against the Germans, said some; an act of foolishness, said others.

It had also been much more than that. As the fighting in Belgium and France raged, many British and Allied soldiers who suffered defeat in battle, but had managed to escape from the advancing German troops, made their way to Brussels. They were still in enemy territory – German-occupied Belgium – but there were rumours of a safe haven at a hospital run by a British nurse. That hospital was the L'École Belge d'Infirmières Diplômées, and the British nurse was 49-year-old Edith Cavell.

Beginning with the first Allied soldiers in November 1914, Edith Cavell set up an escape route that transported these soldiers secretly across the border into neutral Holland; from where they managed to get to Britain. Hundreds of escaped British, French and Belgian soldiers owed their lives to Edith Cavell.

And then, things went wrong. Had there been an informer? Or had German intelligence ferreted out the truth behind the escape route?

Whatever the reason, suspicions had been raised. And on 3rd August Edith Cavell was arrested on a charge of "treason against the German state" and held for questioning at German HQ in Brussels. Five Belgian men were also arrested and were being questioned at another German military base.

For the first eight weeks of her imprisonment, Cavell had been resolute in her refusal to admit to the charges. As Madame Sim had felt, Cavell had argued that, as she was not German but British, therefore she could not be guilty of treason against Germany; only against her own country. And, she further stated, she would never involve herself in any acts that could be interpreted in any way as treason again Britain. Therefore she was not guilty.

Her defence cut no ice with the German commandant, General Herzer. But then, Herzer could not break the resolute Englishwoman down. There was always torture, of course, but Herzer prided himself on doing everything "by the rule book", and if it was revealed that he had tortured Cavell into confessing to helping the Allied soldiers escape, then it might make the validity of any such confession questionable, at least in legal eyes. General Herzer was keen not to be portrayed as someone who resorted to illegal means when obtaining information.

For the last week, Cavell had been kept in solitary confinement in the hope of breaking her spirit, but there was still no sign of a crack in the Englishwoman's manner. If Herzer was going to get the evidence he wanted against Cavell, then he was going to have to use a different method. A confidante. Someone Cavell would see as non-threatening.

"He wants me to get her to talk to me," said Lisette.

The next morning, Lisette stood to attention in General Herzer's office. She had seen the Commandant at a distance; most people in Brussels had. But now, up close, she felt a strong loathing for him. He smelt of perfume. Although he fixed a smile on her, Lisette knew that it was false.

"I am delighted to tell you that you will be employed here as a maid, in the service of Fräulein Cavell," said Herzer. "Has your mother explained your duties to you?"

"Yes," nodded Lisette. "I am to take her her meals, and collect the dishes afterwards. And carry out any errands she wishes me to do for her."

"Excellent," nodded Herzer. He paused, then said: "You know why she is here?"

"Because she is accused of helping soldiers escape," said Lisette.

"*Enemy* soldiers," stressed Herzer. He nodded. "That is so. I have asked you to be her maid because I feel she might need someone to talk to. Someone she knows."

As I thought, Lisette said to herself. *I am to be a spy.*

Herzer leaned forward, so that his face was closer to Lisette's as he said: "It is important that you report to me everything she says."

"About what?" asked Lisette, feigning innocence.

"About everything," said Herzer, standing up straight again. He hesitated, and then once more leaned forward, bending down to breathe his dreadful perfume into Lisette's face. "She may talk to you about the enemy soldiers she helped. If she does, then you must tell me what she says."

"And if she doesn't?" asked Lisette, and she was surprised at her own boldness in challenging the high-ranking and powerful German general this way. *Have I gone too far?* she wondered. *Will he have me arrested for sympathizing with Nurse Edith?*

"If she doesn't," murmured Herzer, "then I would wish you to raise the subject yourself with her."

"You want me to ask her about the soldiers?" queried Lisette.

Herzer nodded. "If she does not offer any information about the matter herself," he said.

Never! thought Lisette. *I will never do that!*

Herzer's next words sent a chill through her.

"Of course," he said, "it may be that you are reluctant to raise the matter with her, for some reason." And this time, when he leaned in to her his tone was harsher, his whisper menacing, as he said: "But if I felt that might be the case, I would ask you to consider the health and safety of your parents. They might also be held as people who have aided and abetted this English nurse."

"My parents are innocent!" burst out Lisette, horrified.

"I am in charge here," snapped Herzer. "I will decide who is innocent, and who needs to be arrested and … interrogated." He smiled, only this time there was not even a pretence of friendliness in his smile. It was malicious – a threatening sneer of a smile. "Remember, your parents' safety is in your hands," he added warningly. "And now, you may take some food to Fräulein Cavell and inform her of your duties." He smiled another cold, icy smile. "I hope she might be pleased at your presence."

As Lisette walked along the corridor, towards the kitchens and away from the Commandant's office, she was filled with rage. The Commandant's threat was blatant: get Edith Cavell to admit to you her part in smuggling the soldiers out of Belgium, or your parents will suffer, possibly die.

I will not betray Nurse Edith, but I have to find a way out of this, thought Lisette. *I have to!*

The guard outside the cell held out his hand to stop Lisette as she approached along the stone corridor – the tray, with a plate of food and a cup of water, held in her hands.

He examined the contents of the tray suspiciously. *Is he looking for a weapon that he thinks I might be smuggling in to her?* wondered Lisette. *If so, he would have difficulty finding one in the plate of potatoes, with a thin piece of meat, and thin gravy.*

Satisfied, the soldier went to the heavy metal door, took out a key and unlocked it, and gestured for Lisette to enter.

Edith Cavell was sitting on a bed, but when she saw Lisette she stood up, a questioning look on her face.

"Good heavens!" she said. "Is that Lisette Sim?"

"Yes, Mam'selle Cavell," said Lisette, walking in and putting the tray down on the small table, as the heavy door was shut and locked behind her.

Cavell smiled.

"You always called me Nurse Edith before," she said. "Even though you are older now, almost a young woman, we can still be friendly, I hope."

"Yes, Nurse Edith," nodded Lisette, and she stood awkwardly to one side, not sure of what to do or say next.

The Englishwoman studied Lisette thoughtfully for a while, then she said: "I heard there was to be a change in the people who would bring me my meals. I must admit, I didn't expect it to be you."

"Nor did I!" Lisette burst out, unable to stop the note of her anger in her voice.

Cavell nodded in gentle understanding.

"Ah yes, of course," she said. "It would have to be someone like you. What did they do? Threaten your parents? How are your mother and father, by the way?"

"They are well," answered Lisette. She threw a wary glance at the door, then gave a quick nod. "Yes," she whispered. "But I will not betray you!"

"Of course you won't," said Nurse Edith. "I know you better than that, Lisette. What does Commandant Herzer want to know? How I helped smuggle soldiers out of Belgium?"

"No!" appealed Lisette. "Please, don't tell me anything!"

Nurse Edith hesitated, then she nodded.

"I will have my meal," she said. "And then we will talk. Of everything, except the War." As she moved the tray nearer to her, she smiled. "I must thank Commandant Herzer for granting me the companionship of a friendly face, even if it is for just a short while."

Then, as Nurse Edith ate, she talked, and encouraged Lisette to talk, asking Lisette what she had been doing since she had last seen her two years before. Lisette talked of how she had been doing at school, and how she had decided to train to be a nurse and follow in the footsteps of Nurse Edith.

"Not exactly in my footsteps, I hope," smiled Nurse Edith. "I would not wish you to be in a place like this. It can be quite damp."

Then it was Nurse Edith's turn to talk. As she had said she would, she avoided talking about anything to do with the War, and instead talked about Lisette going for a career in medicine, and not just as a nurse, but as a doctor. "Because many women would prefer to have another woman as their doctor, rather than some man. We understand how a woman's body works, much more than any man ever can."

As Lisette listened to Nurse Edith talk, she remembered her time in hospital. She had been seriously ill with influenza, not expected to live; but somehow, in between bouts of sleeping and drifting in and out of consciousness, she always remembered Nurse Edith being there by her bedside. Many people said they were terrified of Nurse Edith; that she was hard woman with a sharp tongue; but Lisette had never seen that side of her. Perhaps once or twice, but only when someone had done something dangerously stupid, like the time a trainee nurse had given a patient the wrong medicine. To Lisette, Nurse Edith had been an angel. She owed her life to this woman.

I will not betray you! she vowed fiercely. *I will not!*

For the next two days, Lisette brought Nurse Edith her meals on a tray, and collected her empty plates. After each visit, she was stopped by General Herzer, who demanded: "Has she said anything yet?"

"Only about medicine," replied Lisette.

"I do not wish to hear about medicine," snapped Herzer. "Tomorrow you must ask her directly about the soldiers she helped to escape. Otherwise I will bring your parents in for questioning and ask them why their daughter is refusing to help."

Bring her parents in for questioning. Lisette knew what that meant. When she got home that night she felt sick, so sick that she couldn't eat the dinner her mother laid before her.

"What's up?" asked her mother, worried. "Is everything all right? Are you ill?"

"No," lied Lisette. "Just a little stomach upset. Nothing more. I shall be fine."

The next morning, when Lisette arrived at the Town Hall, she was surprised to find that Nurse Edith's cell was empty, and the door open. A feeling of panic surged through her. Had the Germans taken her out and killed her?

The soldier on guard told her what had happened.

"The English spy has gone to see the Commandant in his office," he said.

"Why?" asked Lisette.

The soldier shrugged.

"Who knows? It was she who insisted."

Lisette hurried up the stone steps to the corridor and headed for the Commandant's office. So, Nurse Edith was in there with the General. Why?

She looked along the corridor. No one else was around. Carefully, she took hold of the door handle and turned it slightly, then a little more, until she felt the latch give. Hardly daring to breathe, she pushed the door with the tips of her fingers, so that it opened the slightest fraction. Not enough to be noticed, but enough for her to hear what was being said inside the office.

Lisette moved to the hard wooden chair placed immediately outside the Commandant's office, kept there for people who were awaiting the General's orders, and sat down. Hopefully, if anyone came along, they would assume she was there waiting to take orders from him.

Edith Cavell's voice came to her, clear and firm. She was angry, but keeping her anger in check, so that her tone was cold and reprimanding. It was the same tone that Lisette had heard her use to that trainee nurse who'd made a serious error. She was putting the General in his place in that same way.

"Your actions have been despicable!" she said curtly.

"Fräulein Cavell—" began the General, but he was cut off.

"Do not interrupt when I am talking!" snapped Cavell. The General fell silent, quelled by the authoritative tone of the Englishwoman. "When I have finished you may make your defence. You have acted with abominable cruelty by making Lisette Sim my maid. We both know why you have done that. You hope that I will talk freely to her about my actions in aiding my country. No doubt you have threatened her, that unless she reports back to you what you want to hear, you will harm her parents."

"I can assure you—!" blustered the General.

"You can assure me of nothing," said Cavell curtly. "Your action has shown me that you are untrustworthy and capable of all sorts of deceit. You are cruel to use this girl in this way. If she tells you anything, it will be on her conscience for ever. And you are quite likely to make things up, anyway. She is terrified of you. You intend to kill me. So be it. I will not let you use this girl and ruin her life. I will tell you what you need to know."

Lisette wanted to run into the office and shout out "No!", but the proud note in Cavell's voice stopped her.

"In fact, I am proud of what I have done. Yes, I managed to get some of *our* soldiers back to England, in order that they would be able to fight again. That was an act of patriotism."

"It was an act of treason against Germany."

"I am not German, I am British. Therefore it was not treason."

There was a pause, then the sound of a rustling of papers, before the Commandant was heard, obviously reading from a document: "The German Military Code states: 'Any person who carries out an act with the intention of helping a hostile power will be deemed guilty of treason.' Paragraph 96 of the Code states: 'This includes conducting soldiers to the enemy.' And Paragraph 160 further states: 'In time of war, this applies to foreigners as well as Germans'."

"That is your law. That does not make it legal."

"The German Military Code has been ratified under the Geneva Convention," defended Herzer. "Under the German Military Code, you are guilty of treason, as admitted by you." There was a pause, then Herzer added: "And under Paragraph 58 of the Code: 'Anyone found guilty of treason, as specified in the Code, will be sentenced to death'."

There was silence from inside the office, broken at last by Herzer saying: "It is your duty to the German State to give me the names of your associates in this act of treason. Will you do that?"

"No," said Cavell firmly. "I am responsible. That is all I will say."

Lisette and her parents stood with a handful of other local people outside the German HQ. It was dawn, and everyone in Brussels knew what was about to happen in the yard at the back of the Town Hall. The English nurse, Edith Cavell, was to be executed by firing squad, along with a Belgian man, Phillippe Baucq, found guilty of working with Cavell to help the Allied soldiers escape.

The German soldiers on duty in the front of the HQ made no

attempt to disperse the small crowd of locals who had gathered. The opposite, in fact: General Herzer had let it be known he would welcome the attendance outside the HQ of any who chose to be there. For him, the execution was an example to others, and the more people who were there to hear it, witness it, the better.

For Lisette, her parents, and the few other locals who had come, their being here was sign of their respect for the British woman and for Phillippe Baucq.

The day after Edith Cavell had proudly told General Herzer what she had done, she had asked Lisette to visit her in her cell.

"There will be no further need for you to act as my maid, Lisette," she said.

Lisette was close to tears as she said: "I heard what you said to the Commandant. You shouldn't have done that. But I know you did it to save me."

Cavell shook her head.

"Don't think that," she said firmly. "I did it for myself. I had already been considering how I should deal with the situation before General Herzer made you my maid. I had decided to tell him, tell the world, what I had done, because I was proud of it. Yes, I will die, but my actions saved the lives of over two hundred Allied soldiers. Those soldiers will return to the War, and they will save the lives of many hundreds more. What is one life, my life, against that?"

The big clock on the Town Hall chimed seven, and from inside the yard behind the building they heard the tramp of heavy boots. Lisette could picture the scene; she had seen that same yard while she had been acting as a maid for Nurse Edith. Three high stone walls, forming an enclosed area behind the Town Hall itself. Four tall wooden posts had been cemented into the floor of the yard for executions.

In her mind's eye, Lisette could see the figure of Edith Cavell walking towards the wooden posts, her back straight, her face firm. Lisette guessed that Phillippe Baucq would be walking alongside her. She didn't know Baucq. She had never met him, or even seen him. But she knew that he must be a brave man, to have done what he had done.

The sound of the heavy marching boots stopped. Orders were shouted in German. Lisette guessed that the soldiers were being assembled into rows. Edith Cavell and Phillippe Baucq would be taken to the wooden posts.

She wondered if they would be tied to the posts, or if they would stand there, taking a position and waiting. Would they accept the blindfolds that were offered to those about to be shot, or would they want to stare at the people who were about to shoot them, let them see the looks in their eyes?

She wondered what Edith Cavell was wearing. Would she be dressed in her nurse's uniform? Or would she be wearing the same clothes she had worn in her cell – the grey dress?

There was more shouting in German from the yard at the back of the Town Hall, and they all heard the loud clicks of many rifles being readied.

Then another shout, and even though it was in German, everyone knew what the order signified: "Fire!"

There was a loud volley as all the rifles fired together. Lisette felt faint, but she forced herself to remain upright. If Edith Cavell could face a firing squad without faltering, then she – Lisette – could remain standing.

A dreadful silence hung over the crowd outside the Town Hall. Lisette's mother had begun to weep, as had some of the others.

And then they all heard a single gunshot – the sound of a revolver.

Why? What had happened? Had Edith or Phillippe Baucq only been wounded by the volley of rifle fire? It seemed unlikely, and yet that one single shot suggested that a final revolver bullet had been needed to finish the execution.

As Lisette turned away with her parents, and headed for home, she vowed: "I will never forget Nurse Edith Cavell. And I will make sure that no one else forgets her, either. When this war is over I will make sure that a plaque is put up on a street somewhere near here, and when I see people look at it and hear them ask: 'Who was Edith Cavell?', I will tell them all about her, and her bravery, and her compassion, and she will live on in people's hearts."

13 October 1915–30 May 1916

Despite last-minute appeals by representatives of the US and Spanish Governments, amongst others, Edith Cavell was shot by firing squad on 12 October 1915. Her execution sent shock and a feeling of revulsion throughout the world, especially in neutral America.

The Germans defended their action by saying that her execution was perfectly legal. She had admitted her actions, and as such was guilty of treason. The fact that she was a woman was irrelevant; she would have been executed if she had been a man; all the Germans were doing was applying equality of punishment.

However, in America, even those who defended Germany's actions during the War realized that by executing Edith Cavell, the Germans had given a powerful propaganda tool to the Allies, and it was one that the Allies took advantage of in their efforts to bring America into the War on the side of the Allies.

After the War, Edith Cavell's body was brought back to England and buried in Norwich. A statue of her was erected in her memory in St Martin's Place, near Trafalgar Square, London. The inscription on the memorial reads: "Patriotism is not enough. I must have no hatred or bitterness towards anyone", which were the words she spoke to the chaplain who called to give her Holy Communion in her cell the night before her execution.

As well as her statue in London, other memorials to her sprang up. Many hospitals were named in her honour across Belgium and England, and around the world, streets and schools in towns and cities were named after her.

Elsewhere, the War raged on. The Western Front remained largely a stalemate, with neither side able to make significant gains.

In November 1915, German and Austrian forces, along with their allies from Bulgaria, invaded Serbia. The Serbian king, Government, and Army, along with many thousands of civilians, fled Serbia and attempted to escape across the Albanian hills to the Mediterranean. Because of blizzard conditions in the high Albanian hills, about 200,000 died of exposure on the journey. A Serbian Government-in-exile was established on the island of Corfu.

In December, the withdrawal began of the British, Australian and New Zealand troops from Gallipoli. Suvla and Anzac Cove were evacuated, with the rest being taken to safety in January 1916.

In January, with the losses at the Front mounting and the Army desperate for more men, the British Military Services Act was passed, bringing conscription to Britain. No longer was the Army to be made up of volunteers; all men from the age of eighteen were to enter the armed forces. A refusal would mean jail, and possibly death by firing squad in extreme cases.

In February 1916, German forces in Cameroon, in Africa, surrendered. But on the Western Front in the same month, the Germans launched a major offensive at Verdun, and captured Fort Douaumont.

In March, Germany expanded its range of enemies by declaring war in Portugal.

So far, the war at sea had been relatively limited: German U-boats had sunk some Allied ships, as well as commercial liners, and the British Navy had had some successes protecting Britain from attack by sea. But all that was about to change, as the biggest sea battle in history was about to take place in the North Sea off the coast of Jutland, near to the coast of Denmark.

Among the combatants was a sixteen-year-old boy, Jack Cornwell, who had volunteered for duty in the Royal Navy, and had trained to be part of a gun crew on a battleship. He was now about to see action for the first time.

Jack Cornwell VC

From the diary of Jack Cornwell, aged sixteen

12 May 1916

I am serving on board HMS *Chester*. The *Chester* has a crew of 402, which means there are lots of men on it crammed into small spaces. You notice it most below decks. There's not much room to hang hammocks, just eighteen inches between each hook, so many hammocks are hung up wherever the men can find a space. At dinner times we cram sixteen to a table, sometimes more, which doesn't give a lot of space for moving your elbows when you are eating.

It's also very hot below decks. Ships like this are built for battle, so there are very few portholes. Also the hull is made of metal, which doesn't let in fresh air like the old wooden hulls used to. There are ventilators on deck, but it's so hot that you don't seem to feel the effect of them much.

Today we were lined up on deck on parade for inspection by Captain Lawson. He's a tall man with a grey beard, very imposing, but – the men say – very fair. He keeps his pet dog on board with him. It's a large sheepdog called Skipper, and when he came to inspect us his dog came with him, following him, and stopping when he did. It almost seemed to be sitting to attention at one point. The men say that the dog is really one of the crew, and the man next to me, Dobby, said afterwards that he thinks the dog actually gets a rum ration.

15 May 1916

Today we did our gun practice. The men with me on my gun are a good bunch, and have worked together before. I'm the only new one in the crew, but they helped me settle in. The man I work with, who sits in the seat controlling the elevation of the gun, is called Patch, and he winked at me as we were preparing.

"Don't worry about getting hurt, son," he told me cheerfully. "Just remember, we're sitting on thousands of tons of explosives. If we get hit we'll all be blown to Kingdom Come and we won't know a thing about it!"

Our gun has thick armour in front of it, which is fixed to the gun and turns with the gun as it moves, so we're protected. One of the gun crew, the shell loader, Batty, doesn't seem convinced by this, though, because he said to me: "It may look safe enough, but see that space below the armour. There's a gap between it and the deck. If shrapnel or something comes under there, it'll take our feet off!"

"Then there'll be no more football for you, Batty!" laughed Patch, and the other men laughed, too. But Batty didn't laugh.

"I've said all along they ought to put something there as better protection," he insisted.

"Stop complaining," our gun leader, Fred, told Batty. "It's just as bad for the Germans on their ships."

"That don't make it any better for us!" protested Batty. "I ain't worried about the Germans. I'm worried about getting home alive, and with my feet! I'm supposed to be getting married when this war's over!"

"And she needs your feet to keep her warm, does she?" chuckled Ned, who was on the traverse controls for the gun.

"I think we ought to stop all this talk about getting killed," said Mick, the ramrodder, sternly. "We don't want to upset the boy on his first day with us."

"I'm not upset," I said. "God's on our side. He'll look after us."

"I'd rather have proper armour right down to the deck floor," insisted Batty, still looking sulky. But then he stopped talking about it, as Mick had told him.

17 May 1916

HMS *Chester* is just one of about fifty ships in the Battlecruiser Fleet. The Battle Squadron, which is even bigger and has the really big battleships, is further north, at Scapa Flow off the Orkney Islands. This is because some of the battleships are so huge they are too big to be anchored at Rosyth, especially at low tide, so they have to stay in deep water.

The two fleets, our Battlecruiser Fleet and the Battle Squadron, are called the British Grand Fleet when they are together. It's such a great name, the Grand Fleet. And it really is grand.

19 May 1916

There are rumours on board that we will be going into battle soon. There have been reports of some of the German Fleet coming out into the North Sea and heading towards Britain for an attack, supported by a whole fleet of U-boats. Everyone on board is glad about the news because we have been stuck here for ages with no sign of going into action, and that makes everyone edgy and tense. We are here because we want to fight!

26 May 1916

In spite of the rumours about us going into action, a week has gone by and nothing has happened. We don't know if the report about the German fleet coming to attack was a true story, or one that someone made up. It's been a month since I left my training barracks at Devonport and I've seen no action at all. All I've done is drill and practise and train. Our gun crew can now work together to load and fire the gun like clockwork, but I want us to do it for real, in a battle against the Germans, not just practising and firing unfused shells into the sea as target practice.

31 May 1916

This is it! At last! We have been given the order to set sail. And not just the *Chester* and the Battlecruiser Fleet, but the whole Grand Fleet! We are going into battle! The word is that we are heading for Jutland. I've never heard of Jutland or know where it is, so I asked Patch.

"Jutland is the northern part of Denmark," said Patch. "They say the German fleet is gathering there ready to make an attack. So we're going out to meet them and stop them."

This morning the order was given to prepare the *Chester* for action, and at half past eleven we weighed anchor and cast off, in convoy with the other Light Cruisers and Destroyers in the Battlecruiser Fleet.

As we passed beneath the Forth Bridge, with our crew standing in lines on the deck, I never felt so proud. Standing there, looking at all the other ships with their crews also standing proudly on deck, with the fleet stretching in each direction port to starboard, and fore and aft, as far as the eye can see. It was an incredible sight. There is nothing like a naval fleet leaving harbour and sailing out to open sea to war. And this is just part of the British Grand Fleet! Once we are out in the North Sea we will be joining with the Battle Squadron, who are steaming south-east from Scapa Flow. We will meet up and head together towards the coast of Denmark, where reports say the German High Seas Fleet has assembled.

Our fleet is hundreds of ships strong! It is hard to put into words how huge and magnificent the Navy is with this many ships all setting out together. We are an armada! We are strong! We are invincible! The British Navy rules the waves!

As we cleared the Firth of Forth, the bugles sounded General Quarters, and we all went below to prepare for action.

Shortly after the bugles sounded again, this time sounding Action Stations. We are going into battle. May God be with us.

It was three o'clock in the afternoon when we met up with the Battle Squadron. We'd been sailing eastwards towards the Danish coast for about three hours, since we left the Firth of Forth. The whole of that time our team had been ready by our gun. I had been standing with my headphones on, waiting for instructions, but so far there had been silence from the Gunnery Officer. All the time I stood there I could feel excitement churning inside me. The Germans were out there! Were they heading towards us, or were they hiding, waiting for us in the rivers of Denmark and Germany?

So far the sea had been calm and the weather good. There was a haze on the sea. It could have been from the effect of the sunlight on the water, but it also could have been from the chimney stacks of the hundreds of ships. Every ship's funnel was pouring out thick smoke, and in this weather it hung lower. One problem is that so many of the ships burn coal, and coal smoke is much thicker than the smoke from ships like ours, which have oil boilers. This thick smoke can make it difficult for the observers who are watching out for the enemy ships, and also for the signallers who have to send messages by flags to the other ships in the fleet.

"The Germans won't come out yet," muttered Ned. "They'll wait till our battleships are with us."

"Why?" I asked.

"Because if they attack us now, they could get cut off by our battleships arriving, and they won't want to be trapped by them. The Germans like a clear run between their ships and the coast so they can run for their rivers."

Just then Batty shouted out: "There they are!"

For a moment I thought he meant he'd seen the Germans, but when I looked I saw our Battle Squadron in the distance, heading towards us. Even from this distance, it was a sight to take your breath away. The really big battleships, the dreadnoughts, were enormous. They made some of the other ships look like toys next to them. To give you an idea of how massive these dreadnoughts were: the displacement of our ship, the *Chester*, was 5,185 tons. Dreadnoughts like *Benbow* and *Iron Duke* had a displacement of 25,000 tons; nearly five times as big as our ship. And I thought our ship was big!

Sailing behind and on either side of the dreadnoughts were more cruisers and destroyers. Hundreds of ships, all ready for battle! It was a sight that filled me with pride. The British Grand Fleet on its way to defeat the Hun, and I was part of it! I wished my dad could see me!

The *Chester* began to turn, and I noticed that the approaching dreadnoughts and the rest of the Battle Squadron were doing the same, and now we were all heading east towards Jutland.

I looked around at the other men on the gun. Patch, Batty, Fred, Mick, Ned, Dobby. Like me, all of them were straining their ears and eyes, looking out towards the horizon, watching for any sign of the German ships. There was a silence on deck. No one hummed a tune, or cracked any jokes, or started telling stories. We were all just watching and waiting. My whole body felt alive, like every nerve-ending was alert and waiting, ready to spring into action as soon as the order was given. But all the time there was nothing. Just our own ships, sailing together, yet at a safe distance apart, and the haze of smoke settling on the sea.

We sailed on for about another hour. The whole time I was alert and tense, standing, waiting, ready. I looked towards the other ships, especially the dreadnoughts, with their hulls painted such a dark grey they almost looked black. The German ships were painted with light grey paint, ours were dark grey, so each side could recognize its own ships and the enemy from a distance.

More time passed. The swell of the sea rose and fell, the waters getting choppier now, but I remained standing, holding onto the gun mounting, ready for action.

Then suddenly we heard it! The sound of heavy gunfire just a few miles distant, towards the south-east!

"We've found 'em!" shouted Patch. "Get ready, boys!"

"Signals," said Fred, pointing at one of the nearest ships, and I saw the flags go up with the orders to us and the other ships around us, ordering us to change direction. We could all feel the ship begin to turn, heading south-east, and gaining speed as it did, pushing towards the German fleet. All the time we could hear the sound of heavy gunfire continuing.

I wondered where the gunfire was coming from? Was it from our own ships or was it from the Germans?

As the ships increased their speed the funnels pushed out more smoke, increasing the haze. I started to pray. *Please God, let me be brave!*

I knew that all I had to do was follow orders and carry out my duties as I had done hundreds of times during training and practice, but it's a different situation when the enemy are firing live shells at you.

I thought of my dad and my brother Arthur fighting in France, and how they would be going through this hour after hour, day after day. Every day, shells falling on their positions and machine-gun bullets flying at them. Now it was my turn.

All the ships had turned south-east now and we were racing onward, the sea rising, the *Chester* catching the wash from the other ships ahead of us.

I could feel a knot in my stomach as I heard the sounds of battle, of big guns firing, and wondered if the rest of the men felt the same. I knew that, whatever happened, I mustn't let them down. I mustn't let Dad down.

I tried to imagine the scene on the rest of the ship. We had trained and practised so many times for Action Stations and Combat, I knew that below decks all steel doors were being shut. The medical parties would be getting ready in the sick bays, setting out surgical instruments, medicines and dressings for wounds. Parties of men that would be carrying out emergency fire repairs would be preparing their equipment: mallets, wedges and boxes of sand.

In the turret and the foretop the Range-finders would be hard at work, getting ready to pin down the position of the enemy ships and work out how fast they were travelling and in which direction, and to pass that information on to the Gunnery Officer, and then on to the gun crews.

Below decks all the steel doors would be locked shut tight with all eight catches instead of the usual two. This would make sure they didn't blow open if there was an explosion.

That was another thing they would be worrying about below decks: a German shell hitting the store of explosives and fuses. If that happened it would blow the ship sky high. That's why the hull of each ship was so heavily armoured.

All this time the thud thud thud of the heavy guns in the distance was getting louder, now accompanied by crashes and explosions, the sound of metal being torn apart, black smoke billowing up in a thick cloud. The battle was raging and the smoke on the water was getting thicker, turning into a fog. We could hardly see those of our ships that were nearest to us, at least, not with the naked eye. We all knew we were far enough away from them for a German ship to slip past.

Now, as we got nearer and nearer to the German ships, I had to fight to keep calm. I looked at the rest of the men in the gun crew. All of them seemed concentrated on manning the gun, getting ready for battle. I wondered if they'd felt the same nervousness as I did when they went into battle for the first time. They'd been joking before, but now all jokiness had gone. I gritted my teeth. I had a job to do. This was no time to start thinking about being afraid.

I continued watching out to sea. My eyes were almost burning now from the strain of peering into the distance, at the ship-filled sea, at the smoke, watching for a ship to appear with a German flag fluttering aloft.

With ships criss-crossing and turning back on their own course, the sea was getting higher, waves lifting and crashing against the side of the *Chester*. I didn't know what the time was, or how long we had been sailing since the bugles had first blown with the order for Action Stations. All I knew was that the enemy was out there, that we were closing on them, and they were closing on us, and already the ships at the head of our fleet were engaged in a full-scale battle.

Suddenly I heard the voice of the Gunnery Officer through my headphones, giving me the elevation for the gun, and I pushed the brass disc to the right marker. Immediately Patch started winding his wheel, bringing the gun down, which meant the Germans were right near us! As Patch stopped winding, Fred pulled the lead connected to the firing pin. There was an almighty BOOMPH!! from the gun and it recoiled as the shell hurtled out from the end of the barrel. At the same time the shell-casing ejected backwards, where Dobby dealt with it, hurling it safely to one side.

Fred opened the breech, the next shell slid into place and Mick pushed it in with his ramrodder. The Gunnery Officer's voice through my headphones ordered me to lower the elevation just twenty points. I changed the setting on the brass disc, and as I did so I saw the German ships appear from out of the black smoke. There were four of them, Light Cruisers, the same as us. I heard a thud from one of them, and saw smoke coming from it, and realized one of them had fired a shell at us. I heard a whining sound and saw the shell getting closer and closer, and then suddenly the deck near me blew up.

There was a flash of white that almost blinded me, then intense heat as flames leapt up, followed by thick black smoke, so thick I couldn't see. I put my hand over my nose and mouth to stop myself choking.

I looked round and saw Ned lying on the deck, a massive hole in his chest where a piece of shrapnel had torn into him, almost cutting him in half.

Suddenly there was another explosion, even louder than the first, right by me, and I heard screaming. The smoke shifted and I could see two men rolling in agony on the deck, and I realized their legs had been cut off just below the knees.

I stood at my post, waiting for instructions over my headphones to set the gun, and I heard a voice say "Six—", and then the rest of his words were lost as another explosion hit us. The whole gun seemed to lift up off the deck with the force of the explosion, as if it was being torn off, and I suddenly realized I'd been hit. I looked down at my front and saw that parts of my uniform had been torn open, shredded across the chest, and I saw the glint of metal among the blue cloth.

At first my body went numb, but then the pain hit me. I'd never felt pain like it. It felt as if my whole body was on fire, as if my skin had been torn off and I was being burned.

I gritted my teeth against the pain. I wouldn't cry out! The Germans wouldn't beat me! Dad and Arthur were suffering this kind of thing every day, and for months and months. If they could take it, so could I.

I was just turning to look at the rest of my gun crew, when there was another BOOOOMPHH!! and an explosion, the force of the blast throwing me back against the metal of the gun. I nearly slipped down, but I managed to grab hold of one of the handles and held on, determined to stay on my feet. I was afraid that if I went down, I'd never get up again, and I had to stay standing. I had to stay by my gun. I was the Sight Setter. Without me the gun couldn't fire at the enemy.

Even though I couldn't see because of the smoke, I knew that the rest of my gun crew were either dead, or badly injured, like me. But I was certain they'd be sending other men to replace them. And when they did, they'd need me as their Sight Setter. I would not desert my post.

The pain was really bad now, like red-hot blades cutting into my chest and my shoulders, but it was my chest where the pain was worst. I looked down at my wounds. The front of my uniform was now soaked in blood and it was sticking to my skin. It sounds stupid but my thought was: "I'm going to have the devil of a job trying to get this uniform clean!"

I can't die, I told myself. *I have to stay alive and stay here for when the others come to take over the gun. I have to stay at my post. I am the Sight Setter. I am needed here.*

I started to feel sick, and I felt dizzy, though whether that was from the smoke or the bits of metal that had gone into my chest, I didn't know. Possibly a bit of both. I could feel myself sagging back against the gun and starting to slide down, but I clenched my teeth and forced myself to stand up. I mustn't sit down. I must keep my eyes open.

All the time I listened, waiting for instructions through my headphones, but I knew the instructions wouldn't come until another gun crew arrived to take over firing the gun. I waited, but no one appeared.

I could hear other explosions from the ship, but further away from my position.

The pain in my chest was getting worse now. It was a dull ache, but if I tried to move, or even coughed, a sharp pain shot through me like a red-hot knife, so I did my best to stay still.

Suddenly I heard footsteps on the deck rushing towards my position. *Another gun crew,* I thought! *We're going after the Germans!* I gritted my teeth against the pain in my chest. I had to hold firm and set the gunsights! But it wasn't a replacement gun crew, they were ship's medics, four of them. Three of them began checking on the bodies of the men lying by the gun, and one of them came over to me.

"Where are you hit, son?" he asked.

"Chest," I managed to say.

He knelt down and examined my chest quickly, and reached out a hand to touch it, but I stopped him with my own hand.

"Hurts," I said, my voice shaking.

He nodded.

"I bet it does," he said.

He stood up and called to the others. "Boy here badly hurt! Looks like shrapnel in his chest!"

One of the other medics came over and joined him, shaking his head. "The others are dead," he announced. To me, he said: "We're heading back to port. We'll get you properly looked at there."

"We can't go back to port!" I protested. "The Germans are here! We have to attack them!"

"We could if we had any guns, and the gunners to fire them," said the man. "But our guns have been shot to bits. The battle's over for us. We're heading to Immingham."

They gave me an injection of something that knocked me out.

When I came to I was lying on the floor of a cabin inside the ship. I still felt pain in my chest, but not as much as I had before. I suppose the injection they gave me had dulled the pain.

I looked down at my body. My uniform had been torn open at the front and a bandage had been wrapped right round my chest and back. It was heavily bloodstained. I saw the bandage was almost flat, so I knew they must have taken some of the pieces of metal out of me; but it felt as if some of them were still there, stuck in my chest. I coughed, and the pain that went through me was awful, like someone had taken a saw to my lungs.

One of the medics was attending to another man, but he heard me cough and got up and came over.

"How are you doing?" he asked.

I opened my mouth to speak, but my mouth was very dry and my throat seemed to have swollen up and I found I couldn't talk. Instead, I gave a slight nod and tried to smile to show him I was all right; even though I knew I wasn't.

"Not long before we get to Immingham," he said. "Then we'll have you sorted out."

"Did …" I stammered, battling to force the words out, "did … we … win?"

The medic's face clouded.

"The battle's still going on," he said. He must have seen the bitter disappointment on my face, because he forced a smile and said: "Don't worry, I'm sure it's going to be all right. Our fleet's bigger than theirs. I've no doubt we've got the Germans on the run. Old Admiral Jellicoe knows what he's doing!"

I tried to smile with him, but a sudden spasm of pain tore through my chest and I coughed, and I saw blood spurt out of my mouth in a spray. Immediately the medic's face looked worried.

"Just hold on there, son," he said. "They'll be able to sort you out at the hospital."

When we arrived at the docks there were ambulances waiting to collect the wounded, like me. I was put on a stretcher and carried to one of the waiting ambulances, and loaded in.

"Won't be long now before we get you to hospital," said the Medical Orderly cheerfully. "You'll see, once we get you there you'll be as right as rain. We'll soon have you fixed up and back fighting the Hun!"

My head felt like it was swimming and all I could feel was pain. Not just in my chest, where the bits of shrapnel had hit me, but all over: my legs, my arms, my head, every part of me felt like it was broken and burning with pain.

I was aware of a face appearing at the door of the ambulance, and I recognized it as being one of the officers, Lieutenant Macfarlane.

"See you keep this boy alive!" he told the MO firmly. "He's a hero! Stayed at his post when the rest of his gun crew were killed. If we had an army and a navy of men with the same sort of guts as him, we'd have won this war before now!"

"I was just doing my duty, sir," I said. At least, I hope I said it, my voice had gone all sort of croaky and I wasn't sure if all my words came out properly.

Then the door of the ambulance slammed shut, and I could feel the vehicle shudder and start to move. And then I passed out.

1 June 1916

I'm in hospital. The nurses tell me this is Grimsby General Hospital. One also told me that we won the battle! The Matron and the officers have told the hospital staff they're not supposed to talk about the battle, or anything about the War, but this one nurse, Nurse Edwards, who's Welsh, says that I deserve to know.

She says she doesn't know the whole story, but from what she's heard from doctors and men who've come in, and some of the telephone calls and other things, she says the Germans retreated to their own ports. She doesn't know how many ships the Germans lost, but she says it looks like the German Navy has been defeated. Britain rules the waves! I smiled when she told me this, then the pain came back again in my chest and I started coughing and there was a lot of blood again, and she ran off to get someone, but I passed out before she got back.

I've been given more medicine, which made my head swim. Nurse Edwards was tidying up my bed and she told me the doctors were going to try and operate on me to get the other bits of metal out of my chest. But just as she said this, another nurse, Nurse Marriner, who was passing told her to shush. Nurse Edwards looked surprised at this, and Nurse Marriner jerked her head and took Nurse Edwards away from my bed so I couldn't hear what they were saying. But I could guess it wasn't good news from the way that Nurse Edwards put her hand to her mouth sharply, and then to her eyes, like she was wiping away tears. Then she hurried out of the ward, and Nurse Marriner came over to me and carried on tidying my bed in place of Nurse Edwards.

"What was all that about?" I asked.

Nurse Marriner gave me a smile.

"Nothing," she said.

"Whatever it was upset Nurse Edwards," I pointed out.

Nurse Marriner smiled again.

"Nurse Edwards gets upset at the slightest thing," she said. "Don't let it worry you."

Then she finished my bed and went on to tidy the next patient's bed.

I lay there for a while, thinking about what had happened. It was true Nurse Edwards did get emotional. I'd only been in the hospital for a short while, and I'd already seen her cry quite a few times. I don't think she was cut out for dealing with men with the sort of injuries suffered in times of war: legs and arms missing, blinded, and lots of them dying right there in the ward.

Then Matron appeared by my bed. She had a different uniform to the other nurses. They wore white and she wore dark blue. I had heard the nurses talk and they all seemed to be scared of Matron. It was like she was their Senior Officer and they were terrified of doing something wrong and upsetting her. But she didn't look terrifying when she came and stood by my bed. In fact, she smiled, and it was a real genuine smile.

"Hello, John," she said.

"Jack," I said, correcting her. Then I thought how rude that sounded, correcting her like that. And what was worse, correcting someone who was a Senior Officer, even if it was in a hospital! I forced a smile, and hoped she'd let me off. "John's my given name but everyone calls me Jack," I explained.

Matron smiled again, which surprised me. From the way the nurses talked about her I'd expected her to tell me off for answering her back.

"Jack," she nodded. "That's a good name. Do you have brothers and sisters?"

I said I did, and I told her about my brothers Ernest and George and Fred and my sister, Lily, and also Arthur and Alice.

"Arthur's fighting with the Infantry in France," I told her. "My dad's there as well, with Lord Kitchener."

"I'm sure they will be very proud of you," said Matron. "I understand you fought bravely in the battle."

"Oh, we carried on all right," I said, remembering what Dad had always told me about not boasting, because no one likes a boaster and a braggart.

Matron smiled again.

"I'm sure you did," she said.

Then she went off. I thought, *She's not as scary as the nurses say at all.*

Later the doctor, Dr Stephenson, came to see me and said: "I know you are a brave boy, Jack. No one could have stayed at his post as you did, as badly wounded as you were, unless they are brave. And, because you are brave and have courage, I know that you will be able to cope with the truth. The fact is, Jack, we can do nothing for you except make you as comfortable as we can. Your injuries are too bad for repair."

I looked at him. He looked so unhappy at having to tell me this.

"So I am going to die?" I asked.

Dr Stephenson nodded.

"I'm afraid you are, Jack."

"How long do I have?" I asked.

"I'm guessing you just have a day, maybe two," he replied. "You are very badly wounded."

I let this sink in. I suppose I had been lucky. I could have been killed along with the rest of the gun crew on the *Chester*. At least I hoped I would have time to say goodbye.

"My ma…" I began.

"A telegram has been sent to her," said Dr Stephenson. "She's on her way to see you."

"Then I shall stay alive until she gets here," I told him.

Dr Stephenson nodded and patted my hand, and then withdrew to go and attend to other patients.

I don't know how long I have been here in the hospital. The nurses give me medicine to ease the pain of my wounds, and it makes me sleep.

There is no clock in the ward so I don't know what the time is when I wake up.

The nurses are very caring to me. They come to me when I am awake and ask me how I feel, and do their best to make me comfortable. I think it is still the same day because every time I woke up I could still see daylight coming in through the windows. Unless I slept the whole night without waking and it is now the next day.

I asked if Ma has arrived yet, but she hasn't. It is a long journey from East Ham in London to here.

When I woke again it was night. The ward was dark except for low lights. I have survived the whole day. The nurses say Ma hasn't arrived yet. I am sure she will come tomorrow. All I have to do is stay alive for the night and get through to the morning. I want to say goodbye to her before I go and let her know how much I love her and Dad. I want her to tell Dad I was thinking of both of them as I lay here, that my last thoughts were of them.

Daylight. I have made it through to the new day. Unfortunately there is a kind of dullness to my eyes and I can't see as clearly as I should. I can see things and people when they are up close, but it's all a bit dim when they are away from me. It feels like there is a weight on my chest the whole time now, and I am having difficulty breathing. The nurses have given me more medicine for the pain in my legs and chest, but they say they can't do much to help my breathing.

It also seems that everything is muffled, as if my ears are blocked. When I was young I once had wax build up in my ears, and Ma cleared it out with warm water, and it came out in a lump and then I could hear properly again. I wonder if I have got wax in my ears again? I can't think why I would get wax all of a sudden like this, so maybe it's something else. I wonder if this is dying? I keep hoping to see Ma, but so far she hasn't come.

Still daylight coming in through the windows. Lots of action in the hospital, nurses hurrying around, lots of sounds of patients coughing and choking and metal basins being put down and picked up and trolleys being wheeled. At least, I think that's what it is. It's all a bit of a muddle of noise. I keep trying to pick out particular sounds, but they all seem to blur into one whooshing sound that keeps coming and going. I can hear voices and I can sort out men's and women's, but I can't recognize who is talking. I keep thinking I hear my mother's voice, but the nurses say she hasn't come yet. It's hard to tell who is who around me. My eyes are dimmer now. I can see it's daylight, but I can't see people's faces clearly. I hope my ma comes while I can still see. I would dearly like to see her face before I die.

Sleep again. Wake again. Sleep again. All the noise seems farther away now. A nurse came and bent over me. I knew it was a nurse because I could smell the starch of her uniform. I hope the same will happen when my ma arrives. I will know her by her smell, and I will be able to see the outline of her face.

The weight on my chest is really heavy now. It's like it's pushing me down onto the bed. I know I can never sit up. My ma will have to lean right over me for me to see her, but I will know she is here. All I have to do is hang on. She will be here soon, I know.

Someone touched me and I woke up.

"Ma?" I said. "Is that you?"

"Not yet," said a woman's voice, and I knew it was a nurse.

I tried to sit up, but the weight on me was too heavy.

"Give Ma my love," I said. "I know she's coming."

2 June–14 September 1916

"Give Ma my love. I know she's coming" were Jack Cornwell's last words. He died on 2 June 1916. Unfortunately, the telegram informing his mother, Lily, of Jack's injuries didn't arrive until it was too late. By the time she reached Grimsby, Jack was dead.

Jack Cornwell was sixteen years old when he died, and he was awarded Britain's highest military medal, the Victoria Cross, for his bravery.

The Battle of Jutland – which took place in the North Sea off the coast of Denmark, between the British Grand Fleet and the German High Seas Fleet – is considered by many naval historians to be the biggest sea battle there had ever been since Henry VIII's time. Bigger even than Trafalgar, or the defeat of the Spanish Armada, it was the last great naval battle. All other sea battles afterwards were dominated by the addition of aircraft.

The two opposing fleets were huge: The British Grand fleet (commanded by Admiral Sir John Jellicoe – second in command: Admiral Sir David Beatty) consisted of 28 battleships, 9 battlecruisers, 8 armoured cruisers, 26 light cruisers, 78 destroyers, 1 minelayer, and 1 seaplane carrier. The German High Seas Fleet (commanded by Admiral Reinhard Scheer – second-in-command: Admiral Franz Hipper) consisted of 16 battleships, 5 battlecruisers, 6 pre-dreadnoughts, 11 light cruisers, and 61 torpedo boats.

But it wasn't just the number of the ships, it was their size and construction. The battleships, especially the dreadnoughts, were unlike anything ever seen before. Huge iron ships, replacing the wooden ships that had sailed the seas for centuries.

The final casualties, both in shipping and men, were as massive as the two respective fleets. In the British Fleet, 6,094 men were killed, 510 wounded, and 177 captured; in the German Fleet, 2,551 were killed with 507 wounded. The British Fleet lost 3 battlecruisers, 3 armoured cruisers and 8 destroyers. The German Fleet lost 1 pre-dreadnought, 1 battlecruiser, 4 light cruisers, and 5 torpedo boats. The total tonnage sunk was: British Fleet, 113,300 tons; German Fleet, 62,300 tons.

Afterwards the British Government did their best to hush up the Battle of Jutland. Until mid-June 1916 the British public was not even allowed to know there had been a great sea battle in the North Sea. Officers and men who had taken part in the battle were ordered not to mention it. Finally, as rumours that a battle had taken place circulated from Germany and Holland, the Admiralty were forced to issue a press statement in which they grudgingly admitted that there had been a "naval engagement" off the Jutland coast. Why the secrecy? Because the British losses, both in ships and men, had been so high that the Government were worried that it would be seen as a failure. The losses of the huge battlecruisers *Queen Mary, Invincible* and *Indefatigable*, all destroyed with all hands. Three thousand men dead in those three sinkings, with more than 3,000 British dead among the rest of the British Fleet.

But the Battle of Jutland marked the end of the German Navy. After Jutland, the German Fleet retreated to German waters, and remained there until the end of the First World War.

Meanwhile, on the Western Front, one of the bloodiest battles in the history of warfare was about to begin: the Battle of the Somme.

It was planned as a major assault by the armies of the French and British Empires against the German front lines, and was launched on 1 July. That first day of the Battle saw combined French and British forces victorious at Foucaucourt-en-Serre, just south of the River Somme; but at the same time as this victory forced the Germans back, further along the front line, between the Albert-Bapaume Road and Gommecourt, the British attack failed against strong German resistance. With 60,000 British casualties in that one day, it was the worst day in the history of the British Army.

Throughout the rest of July and through August, a series of bloody battles raged all along the Somme, with the Allies attacking and the Germans defending. The Allies were desperate to break through the enemy lines, but there were no breakthroughs; just temporary victories forcing the enemy back a short distance, where they rallied and launched a counter-attack. It seemed that any ground each side made appeared to be lost in the days and weeks that followed.

September 1916 at the Battle of Flers-Courcelette saw the third and final offensive of the Somme mounted by the British and French armies. This battle saw the first appearance on the Somme of troops from Canada and New Zealand. It also saw the introduction of a new weapon ... the heavy tank.

The Somme: tanks and conchies

15 September 1916

"Conchies!" spat Bill Merton angrily. "I hate 'em!"

Eighteen-year-old Jack Henry looked towards where Bill, the tank driver, was looking. A group of men in army uniforms were loading supplies into a field ambulance. On the canvas side of the ambulance a large red cross had been painted, and the men wore armbands with the same symbol.

Jack, Bill and the rest of the crew of the Mark I tank were taking a last breath of fresh air before they climbed aboard the monstrous metal machine. It was dawn, and all around them were scenes of activity, the preparations for an attack: soldiers with rifles and fixed bayonets and steel helmets, waiting in their trenches; the big guns lined up behind, ready to launch their huge shells against the German lines, and the field ambulances, ready to move into action, the stretcher bearers to pick up wounded soldiers and carry them to the ambulances and take them to the field hospital.

"How do you know they're conchies?" asked Jack, curious. "They just look like army medics to me."

Conchies. Conscientious objectors. Men who refused to carry

weapons, or play any active part in the War. Most conscientious objectors were still back in England, working as labourers on farms; and some who refused to do even that were often sent to prison, where they suffered harsh treatment from both the warders and other prisoners because they were viewed as traitors. Some had been sent to the front to act as stretcher bearers on the battlefield. But the group setting up the improvised medical station and loading equipment onto the field ambulances looked no different to the regular army medical units.

"I heard someone talking about 'em," growled Bill. "They ain't just medics, they call themselves the Friends Ambulance Unit, that's who they are."

"So?" asked Jack, still none the wiser.

Bill spat again and let out a snort.

"Don't you know nothing?" he demanded. "Friend is what Quakers calls themselves. Rotten pacifists! Cowards!"

"They can't be that much of cowards, or they wouldn't be here," countered Jack. "They're still getting shot at, same as we are."

"No they ain't, and that's the point!" retorted Bill hotly. "The Germans see them with their big red crosses, and they leave 'em alone."

Jack shook his head.

"That don't work when it's a shell from a big gun," he pointed out. "They fire them from a mile away. The gunners can't see whether someone's got a red cross on them or anything, they just aim them at our lines."

Bill glared at Jack.

"You defending them?" he demanded aggressively. "You defending cowards and traitors?"

"No," said Jack. "I'm just making the point that they're out here picking our blokes up when they get wounded, and they have just as much chance of getting killed out here as we have."

"No they haven't!" snapped Bill firmly. "When the whistle blows, they don't go on the attack." He shook his head. "And if I get wounded and one of those conchies comes and tries to patch me up, I'm telling him to get lost! I won't have any coward and traitor laying his hands on me!"

Then they heard the shrill sound of the whistles blowing, calling them to action.

"That's it," said Bill. He turned to the rest of the tank's crew, who were sucking in deep lungfuls of air to counter the foul atmosphere they were about to encounter inside the tank, and shouted: "Time to get on board!"

Jack pulled his mask made of leather and chainmail over his face, and put his leather helmet on his head. He kept his gas mask hanging around his neck. There wasn't much room inside the body of the tank, and with all the bits of metal sticking out inside it, there was a chance of banging your head against them and getting injured. The mask was to protect against bullet splash, or fragments being knocked off the inside of the hull. These tanks were still a very new and experimental weapon, and things like the mask and the helmet had been brought in as a result of incidents on the test drives, when soldiers inside the tank had been badly injured.

All along the line, the crews of the other forty tanks lined up for the attack were climbing aboard their vehicles.

For Jack, the worst thing about the tank was the noise and the air. Or, rather, the lack of air.

There was no dividing wall between the crew and the tank's engine. This meant that the crew breathed in carbon monoxide, as well as fuel and vapour from the engine, as well as cordite fumes from the tank's weapons. Once the engine had started up, the heat inside the tank could reach 120 degrees, 50 degrees centigrade in continental temperatures, and quite a few crews had been found unconscious inside their tank, overcome by heat and fumes.

Because of the noise, radio contact was impossible, so communications with command post was carried out by carrier pigeon. Each tank carried two pigeons in small cages, and each pigeon had its own tiny exit hatch. If an urgent message needed to be sent, then a small piece of paper was slipped into the tube attached to the pigeon's leg, and it was released through its hatch. The hope was that any pigeon with a message from HQ for the tank crew would be able to find its particular tank. Ruefully, Jack reflected that this system of communication wasn't to be depended on. The truth was, once they were in their tank and rolling into battle, they were on their own.

How would the tank cope? Jack wondered as he took his seat inside the hull, by the gears. Jack was one of two gearsmen. So far, all they had done was train on the tank. None of these machines had actually gone into combat against the enemy – today was the first time. Today would show if the promise of these "wonder machines that would win the War" was true; or if – as had happened so often during training – the heavy machines would get bogged down in mud and remain stuck there, an easy target for the Germans.

If that happened, the big danger was a German shell, or even a bullet, striking the fuel tanks, which were at the front and top of the tank, right above the heads of the crew. If that happened and the burst fuel tank ignited, there was a very good chance they would all die, burn to death. There was only one hatch for the whole crew to get in and out, and that hatch was in direct line of any burning fuel from the fuel tanks.

He remembered when he told his pal, Ed, that he'd been chosen to train for a tank crew.

"You lucky so-and-so!" Ed had said. "Safe inside one of them big metal machines, while we're out in the open, getting shot at!"

At least, out in the open, there was a chance of escape, thought Jack. The tank was huge, and heavily armoured, it was true, but that also made it a perfect target for the German big guns.

The tank was operated by two drivers and two gearsmen. Bill was the senior driver, and also the commander of the tank crew. He operated the brakes. The other driver operated the primary gearbox. The drivers communicated with the gearsmen by using hand signals to change direction, or to alter the speed – though the tank didn't ever move faster than walking pace.

There were *some* small openings in the tank's hull: the observation port at the front of the tank through which Bill could see to steer; and the gun hatches for the two big six-pounder guns and the three 8-mm Hotchkiss machine guns. But these hatches were very small, to cut down the chance of the enemy being able to fire through them. Basically, once you were inside and the tank was in action, you breathed engine fumes.

Bill gestured with his hand, and Jack and Bert, the other gearsman, pulled on their levers to set their tracks rolling. The Mark I had two separate metalled tracks, with each of the two gearsmen operating one of the tracks. By stopping one of the tracks while the other rolled, the tank could turn. Right now, Bill was taking them dead ahead, straight towards the German lines.

Jack felt the hull of the tank shudder, but whether it was from the motion of the huge engine, or the rumble of the tracks, or the German guns, he couldn't tell. It was all noise and vibration.

The tank could go where other vehicles couldn't. It could cross trenches, crush barbed wire and ride over mud – provided the mud wasn't too deep.

Jack could imagine the scene outside: the row of tanks lumbering forward at the front of the attack, with lines of soldiers following behind them, using the tanks as shields.

He wondered if the Germans were aware of these new inventions, the tanks. Their development had been kept a strict secret, even the name of the machine, "tank", had come about because the boffins who'd created them had referred to them in all plans and documents as "water tanks" in an effort to stop the Germans finding out about them, and what they were.

Jack doubted if that would have stopped the Germans from finding out about these new weapons. It seemed that the Germans always knew what the Allies were up to.

The tank rolled on, the engine vibrating and burning, the gears and brakes crashing, the whole machine shaking and shuddering. Jack wondered how long had passed since they first started rolling. Were they anywhere near the German lines yet? It was no use asking Bill, even if he could see through his tiny observation hole at the front, he couldn't say anything that could be heard.

Jack kept his eyes on Bill's hands, watching for the signals, pulling at the levers to change direction, to slow or speed up his track, and watched Bert do the same. Sweat poured down his face from beneath the leather of his helmet, blinding him, but he blinked it away, concentrating hard.

Concentration. That what survival here was all about – concentration, following instructions, working as a team.

The tank rolled on, but the next time it shook and shuddered, Jack knew that there had been an explosion just outside. Even over the noise of the engine there had been that distinctive WHUMPPP!!!, the sound adding to the noise inside the tank. Had it been a direct hit? Were they damaged? Apparently not, because after a minute to get itself back on track, the tank moved on, rocking up and down as it did so.

We must have reached a trench, thought Jack. It was so frustrating, not being able to see what was happening, or even work it out from sounds.

The vehicle shook again, rocking sideways this time, and Bill raised a hand to call for Jack to slow down his track to bring the tank round, and back on track.

Jack saw a flash of light blossom around Bill's head, and realized that an explosion had gone off just outside, right near to Bill's observation port. Bill raised his hand to call for a manoeuvre, and at the same time the tank's machine guns opened fire; but then another blossom of light flared, and this time Bill slumped down in his seat and then lolled back, his arms hanging loosely down.

Jack reached out an arm and slapped the leg of the nearest machine gunner, and gestured towards Bill's body; then pointed at the levers by his own position.

The machine gunner nodded and slipped into Jack's empty seat as Jack twisted his way through the tight quarters of the tank to Bill.

Bill wasn't dead, but he was unconscious. A sliver of shrapnel had burst through the small observation aperture and into him, beneath his collarbone, not far above his heart. He was losing blood fast.

Suddenly there was an even louder crunching noise than before from the gears, and then the tank shuddered to a halt. The gears kept racing and the engine pounded away, but there was no movement, apart from a rocking from side to side. The tank had stalled. Either the gears had broken down, or perhaps the tracks had been blown up and torn apart, but the tank wasn't moving. They were stuck.

Suddenly, among the smells of carbon monoxide and cordite, Jack's nose picked out another: the smell of fuel. He looked up, and saw the drip drip drip of fuel coming from above him. The fuel tank had been hit and ruptured. A shell or, even a bullet, striking the liquid would set it off, and within seconds they would be trapped inside a blazing metal box.

Jack reached out and slapped the arms of the two men nearest to him to get their attention, and pointed at the dripping fuel, and at the hatch. Then, he stood up and released the catch of the hatch and pushed upwards.

The sudden rush of air made him feel dizzy, as it often did when the hatch was finally opened, but he reached down, grabbed Bill beneath his arms and began to haul him upwards.

Bert joined him, and together they propped the unconscious Bill against the short ladder that led up from the hull to the hatch. Jack clambered over Bill to the hatch opening, and then reached down, grabbing hold of Bill. Bert got beneath Bill, and together they managed to slide Bill's limp body up the short ladder, and then to the actual opening.

Jack climbed out of the hatch, and as he did so bullets pinged off the metal of the tank and ricocheted around him. One bullet flew upwards past him, and he felt a thump as it struck his leather helmet.

We can't go back inside and hide, thought Jack. *We'll burn to death if we do. I might get shot, but this way there's a chance.*

Jack used all his strength to pull Bill's heavy body out through the hatch, with Bert pushing upwards from inside, and finally Jack found himself tumbling down from the tank and landing heavily in the mud, with Bill on top of him.

All the time, the tank was rocking and shuddering, and Jack saw that it was listing dangerously to one side, towards him.

If it rolls over now, I'm dead, thought Jack.

He began to drag Bill away from the tank, through the mud, but it was so deep that even as he tried to move, he sank in the thick clay mud up to his knees, the mud holding him, gripping him, pulling him down.

Then there were splashes beside him as first Bert, and then the rest of the crew, tumbled out through the hatch and landed in the mud, and joined Jack in dragging Bill's body away from the tank.

They were just in time.

There was an explosion above them, and flames fell down around their position, some of the burning flakes of metal landing on their clothes. Jack immediately rolled himself in the mud, smothering the flames, as did the others. Then they carried on dragging Bill away from the burning tank. Jack could feel the heat from the tank as the blaze took hold, flames pouring out through the open hatchway above them.

In spite of the noise of the still-running engine, and the crackling of flames, Jack was also aware of the noise of bullets striking the body of the tank. The Germans were still firing at them.

Suddenly Bert collapsed, falling face forward in the mud.

Jack moved to him, fighting his way through the mud that was doing its best to hold him back. He turned Bert over, and saw at once that he was dead. Beneath his leather and chainmail mask, Jack saw Bert's face, his eyes open and staring, but seeing nothing. There was a dark stain on the front of his uniform. He'd been shot through the heart.

More bullets hit the tank, bouncing off its metal body.

Jack saw that the others had managed to drag Bill's body clear of the burning tank, and then he was aware of movement above him. He looked up, and saw that the mass of the tank had slipped further to one side in the mud, and was now rolling … towards him!

Frantically, Jack scrambled up on top of the mud and slid, almost as if he was trying to swim over the surface, and as he did so he felt the earth shake behind him. It was like an earthquake, a massive tremor. He kept sliding and swimming over the surface of the mud, and when he reached the other members of his crew he stopped and looked back.

The huge tank had collapsed half on its side, and was lying half in, half on the mud, flames and thick black oily smoke pouring out from the open hatchway.

"We'll take him!" yelled a voice.

Jack turned and saw that two stretcher bearers were struggling their way through the mud towards them. They laid the stretcher down on the mud, put Bill's unconscious body on it, and were just turning to take him away, when one of the stretcher bearers collapsed over the stretcher. He'd been shot, and Jack could see he'd died instantly.

Jack struggled through the mud and eased the dead body of the stretcher bearer off Bill, then took the handles himself. He nodded at the other stretcher bearer, and together they began to push their way through the mud, doing their best to keep the heavy stretcher level. The rest of the tank crew joined in, lending their hands and support, sharing the load. As they neared the field ambulance, other medics came to join them, taking the stretcher from them.

Jack watched them load the stretcher into the ambulance, and drive off. Then he turned and looked back towards the still burning tank, and the dead body of the field medic. Bert was there too, out of sight, his body buried beneath the collapsed tank.

It was another four days before Jack was able to check on Bill. He was still in a field hospital, but patched up.

"How's it going?" he asked as Jack walked into the ward and sat down on the end of his bed.

"Much the same as it was before," said Jack. "They've given us another tank. We go out in it tomorrow."

"Another assault?"

"Of course," said Jack.

"I heard about Bert," said Bill.

Jack nodded.

"And … the medic," added Bill, awkwardly. He let out a big sigh. "I was wrong."

"About what?" asked Jack.

"About the conchies. He was a conchie, wasn't he?"

"Yes," said Jack.

"And he came out and died saving me?" said Bill.

"Yes," said Jack again.

"Who was he, do we know?"

"No," said Jack.

"Can you find out?" asked Bill. "Just his name. Only I'd … I'd like to write a letter to his family. To say thanks, and tell them how brave he was." He shook his head. "He wasn't a coward."

"No," said Jack. "He wasn't."

16 September–11 October 1916

Of the fifty British Mark I tanks that went into action on 15 September at Flers-Courcelette, only nine actually managed to penetrate the German lines. Most of the others broke down, or became stuck in the muddy terrain. However, these massive war machines did give an army an enormous psychological advantage, and it was decided to continue to develop the tank as a weapon of war; and in particular to deal with the technical problems that had plagued the original Mark I.

For their part, the French developed their own version of the tank during this same period, 1915–1916, while Germany didn't begin production of tanks until 1918, when the War was nearing its end.

Conscientious objectors were those people who, on religious or moral grounds, took a pacifist view and refused to take up arms against another person. Around 17,000 men were recorded as refusing to fight on the grounds of conscience, or religious principles. Most were sent to work on farms, as the production of food was vital, or were sent to the front to work as stretcher bearers.

One of the most high-profile faith groups to adopt a position of conscientious objection to military action were the Quakers, who had always followed a pacifist philosophy. However, a thousand men, mostly Quakers, volunteered for the Friends' Ambulance Unit, a volunteer ambulance service that operated on the front line in France and Belgium from 1914 to 1918. They did not carry weapons, but worked as a non-combatant medical unit.

By now, the War had been going on for two years, and with no sign of victory for either side, the morale of the troops on the Somme was being worn down.

The Somme: Oberndorf

17 October 1916

Nineteen-year-old Private Gunter Beck sat with his comrade, Karl Waldheim, in the small cave they had dug out of the thick clay wall of their trench. It was their protection and their home, a place of shelter when it rained, as it seemed to do all the time lately. Sometimes there could be as many as six or eight soldiers crammed into the cave, lounging on one of the three armchairs that had been ransacked from a nearby ruined building, two of them broken with the stuffing poking out of the cushioning. Another two chairs had been made out of wooden crates. But today there was just Gunter and Karl. And as Gunter reread the letter from his sister, Anna, he wished for once that Karl, his friend since childhood, wasn't there.

As he read the letter again his eyes filled with tears, making it difficult to read; but he knew what it said, he had memorized every word during that dreadful first reading.

Oberndorf am Neckar

Germany

13 October 1916

Private Gunter Beck

27th Infantry Regiment

IV Army Corps

My dearest brother,

I write to you with most dreadful news.

Yesterday, British and French planes attacked the Mauser rifle factory in our town. They came out of nowhere in the middle of the day, so many of them I couldn't count them.

Our brave German pilots went up in their fighter planes to try and defend the Rifle Works, but we only had a few planes against so many of the enemy.

I was at home looking after Mother – you know she has not been well since Father died – and I went out into the garden to watch them. Mother screamed for me to come indoors, telling me I would get killed if I stayed out, but I could not go in, I stayed out in the garden as if hypnotized by the sight of what was happening in the sky.

And then, horror of horrors, the bombs began to rain down from the enemy planes. All I could think of was our dear sister, Liesl, at work at the factory, and think "Why are they attacking our factory? Those are not soldiers in there. They are ordinary working people. This is wrong."

But still the bombs came down. The air was filled with loud explosions and smoke and fire.

Many were killed. Among them – and tears come to my eyes again as I write these words – our own dear Liesl.

The tragedy has put Mother to bed. She is in shock, but Dr Ebbe says he thinks it will pass, as it did after Father died.

There is another tragedy: another dear friend of ours who died in the attack was Helga Waldheim. This made everything especially hard, because you know Helga was like another sister to us, as well as being Liesl's best friend.

And now, dear brother, I need to ask you a favour. Will you tell Karl?

Frau Waldheim is too ill to write the letter to Karl telling him his sister has died, and Dr Ebbe has asked me if I will write to you to tell you of the tragic news, and to ask if you will tell him. You and Karl have been friends since childhood, and Dr Ebbe knows that you and Karl are serving in the same unit together.

Will you tell him the bad news: that his sister, poor dear Helga, is dead – and so is our own dear sister Liesl, his beloved fiancée.

We are a family united in grief and tragedy.

Your loving sister,

Anna

"It must be bad news," said Karl quietly, his voice showing his concern for his friend.

Unable to speak, Gunter nodded. Instead, he held out the letter to Karl, who took it and began to read.

Gunter turned his head away and concentrated on looking at the wall, at the attempts at decoration they had made, putting up pictures, nailing cartoons to the wooden struts that held up the clay walls and roof. Then he heard the first groan from Karl, and then a low moan, and finally a howl.

The sound was unnerving. It wasn't even human; it was that of an animal in pain.

Gunter turned.

Karl was still sitting in the chair, but now he was on the edge of it, tears streaming down his face.

Gunter reached out and tried to take the letter back, but Karl's fingers were gripping it tightly, almost as if he was desperate to hold onto it, like a drowning man clings grimly to a lifebelt.

Gunter let go of the letter; he would take it back from Karl later.

Karl's eyes closed, and he bit his lip in an effort to stop himself from crying out. Then he whimpered, and began muttering. Gunter heard the names Liesl and Helga, and then the word "dead" repeated over and over again.

"Crying will not help, Karl," said Gunter. "We must be men."

"I must go home," said Karl. "I must be with Mother. She has no one with her."

"Anna will be with her," said Gunter.

Karl shook his head.

"I have to go home. I need to be there when they bury Liesl and Helga."

"We cannot go home," said Gunter. "We are here to win this war."

"We cannot win this war," said Karl mournfully. "No one can win this war. We go nowhere. We will all die here, and no one will win."

"Sssh!" said Gunter sharply, and he shot a hasty look towards the entrance of the cave to make sure that no one was around to hear Karl's words. "Such talk is treason."

"It is the truth," said Karl, and he began to cry again, his tears falling on the letter in his hand. "I have to go home. We should all go home."

"And how will you get home?" demanded Gunter, trying to bring some reason back into the conversation. He, too, was devastated at the loss of Liesl, and also of Helga, but he realized that he had to be strong for Karl, show courage. "They will not transport you home unless you are wounded. And even then, you would not go home. You would be put into a hospital until you are well enough to return to the Front. You cannot go home, Karl. Not until this war is over."

Karl shook his head and waved the letter at Gunter.

"This war is over," he said. "I am going home."

"How?" insisted Gunter, hoping his question would bring about an end to this state that Karl had descended into.

"I will walk home," replied Karl simply.

Gunter stared at his friend and realized with a shock that the letter had made Karl mad. His friend had lost his sanity.

He leaned forward and put his hand on his friend's knee and patted it comfortingly.

"Karl, you cannot," he said. "They will not let you."

"They will not see me," said Karl. "I will be a ghost, walking through the lines." He waved his arm towards the entrance of the small cave. "We are surrounded by ghosts. One more will not be noticed."

What can I do with him? wondered Gunter desperately. *Should I call an officer and tell him what has happened, that Karl is suffering? But if I do that, they will shoot Karl for treasonable talk and desertion.*

"Karl…" he began, his voice awkward, hesitant, but Karl was already talking, ignoring Gunter, in a world of his own – lost in thoughts of anger and bitterness.

"We have been in this same trench, or one just like it, for over a year, ever since we volunteered," Karl continued. "We have advanced a few metres, we have retreated a few metres, and each time we end up in a trench just like this. It has been this way since this war began. We know this from the older soldiers who have been here since the beginning."

"It was never going to be an easy victory," defended Gunter.

"They told us it would be over by Christmas last year. They told the first soldiers who marched into France that it would be over by Christmas in 1914."

"We have to hang on," said Gunter. "We are fighting for our country."

"We are *dying* for our country," stated Karl flatly. "We are dying in such vast numbers there is no time to bury our dead." He gestured at the walls of the small cave. "The walls here are held up by bones and skulls of dead soldiers. It is the same with the trenches. The dead lie where they are fallen, or are pushed into the walls, and there they rot, their flesh decomposing and eaten by rats, until just the bones are left. This is not the way it should be. Even in the old days, there were pauses in the battle to give time for the dead to be buried with honour."

"It is the same for the British and the French," countered Gunter. "They, too, live with their dead in their trenches. We have seen that, when we have made an advance into their front lines."

"And we have left our dead behind in their trenches when we have retreated," said Karl. "Their dead and our dead, side by side, rotting in the mud." He shook his head and he handed the letter back to Gunter, who took it and put it quickly into the pocket of his tunic, as if afraid that Karl would snatch it from him again.

"I shall walk home," he repeated.

"You will not," said Gunter firmly. Then, to his own surprise, Gunter pulled his revolver from its holster and levelled it at Karl. "I will shoot you before that happens. You are no coward, Karl, and I will not have that said of you, and your name insulted. Because that is what will happen if you try and run away home."

Karl studied the pistol in Gunter's hand, his expression puzzled.

"You would shoot me?" he asked.

"Yes," said Gunter.

Karl fell silent, studying his friend quizzically, as if weighing up whether Gunter really would carry out his threat. Finally, he gave shrug, and then a half-smile.

"In that case, I will stay," he said.

Gunter felt a surge of relief go through him. Would he really have shot his best friend, someone he'd known since they were just small boys of four years old? He didn't know. He hoped not, but at the same time he hoped he would have, rather than have his friend named as a coward.

Suddenly there was a huge explosion that shook the walls of the cave, and then another. If it hadn't been for the wooden supports keeping up the roof and walls, the whole lot would have collapsed on them, burying them. As another explosion rocked the earth, they heard the shrill blast of a whistle from outside, and then Wilhelm Root burst in, bending low as he thrust his way into the cave.

"The enemy are attacking!" he shouted. "Quick! We are called to action!"

Gunter pressed himself against the edge of the trench, sighting along his rifle towards the enemy. Next to him was Karl, like Gunter, half-lying on the clay, half-standing. Gunter had snatched up Karl's rifle and pressed it into his hands, and like an automaton, the result of training and drill and carrying out orders without thinking, Karl had joined with Gunter and Wilhelm and their other comrades in the rush to the edge of the trench, the top of the earth wall laid with sandbags, where they took up their defensive positions.

Ahead of them was No Man's Land, a wide and deep stretch of open land, a quagmire of mud and tangled barbed wire, and corpses and stray human bones. As Karl had said, neither they nor the enemy had had time to bury their dead. Men lay where they fell, and decomposed or were eaten by rats.

The barrage from the enemy's big guns, shelling their positions, had been the signal that an offensive was about to take place. The enemy always did that: tried to smash the trenches, kill as many soldiers as possible, destroy the German defences with their huge shells to pave the way for the infantry to attack. In the early days of the War that technique might have worked, but the Germans had been in these trenches for so long they had fortified them: cement and concrete bunkers, as well as the dug-out caves. A direct hit might destroy a bunker or collapse a cave, but mostly the clay soil absorbed the impact. The big danger was shrapnel, small sharp dangerous pieces of metal flying at speed out from the explosion, tearing flesh, smashing bones in two, slicing off a face or a hand. Some men had been completely obliterated by shrapnel, their bodies left as scattered blobs of meat and bone.

Gunter peered ahead at No Man's Land. The smoke from the enemy's big guns was drifting towards them. Or was it gas? But, if that were the case, then the enemy would be wearing gas masks, and as Gunter saw the outlines of the first enemy soldiers appearing through the smoke, rifles and bayonets pointing forward, he saw that they were not wearing gas masks. A straightforward attack, then. Another suicide offensive launched.

These soldiers were French, he could see that from the distinctive shape of their helmets, and their uniforms. Row upon row of them, advancing across No Man's Land.

Gunter took aim at the front row and fired, and saw a French soldier topple and fall. One down.

Beside him, Karl was firing. Another French soldier collapsed.

The sound of a machine gun started up further along the line, clatter clatter clatter clatter, and more French soldiers fell.

Why do they come on when they are walking to certain death? thought Gunter. *Because they are soldiers obeying orders. We do the same.*

The French were firing now, bullets striking the sandbags and the earth, sending mud and small stones flying up in Gunter's face.

A grenade was thrown, landing in the trench just along from Gunter's position. There was a scramble to get away from it, then it exploded, the flash and force of it knocking soldiers over. There were screams followed by moans of pain.

Some soldiers fell against Gunter, but he ignored them, just kept firing. As did Karl.

Good old Karl, Gunter thought. *He has come through. He fights as bravely as ever, defends his position.*

A bullet from the advancing French struck Gunter's helmet, the force of it knocking him backwards and sending him tumbling down from his foothold into the trench itself. He landed on the wooden duckboards and sprawled half-in half-out of a pool of wet mud, but still hanging onto his rifle. He pulled himself up, and then began to climb back up to his position. As he did so, a figure fell, landing on him, and then tumbled down onto the duckboards, arms spread wide, mouth and eyes open, a bullet hole where the middle of his face should have been.

For a second Gunter thought it was Karl, but then he realized it was Wilhelm Root.

Gunter hauled himself back up, and into his position on the trench wall.

Through the sounds of firing and shouting and yelling came the sound of two shrill blasts on the commander's whistle, taken up and repeated down the line by the whistles of junior officers.

Fix bayonets!

Gunter took his bayonet from his belt and slotted it on the barrel of his rifle, fixing the catch to secure it in place. He cast a quick look towards Karl, and was relieved to see that he was doing the same. Going into action was the best thing for Karl.

Three blasts on the whistles sounded along the line. Over the top! Hand-to-hand combat.

Gunter began to climb up the steps cut into the clay to where the sandbags formed the defensive wall at the top. Along with hundreds of his comrades he hauled himself over, out of the trench.

The French soldiers were still coming, rifles firing, and now they were also using their rifle barrels and bayonets to hack at the barbed wire. Some were holding wooden boards, and they threw these down onto the barbed wire and stomped across them, driving the barbed wire down into the mud.

Gunter moved forward towards the advancing French troops, firing his rifle, reloading, firing again. The air was thick with smoke from the guns and the smell of cordite. Karl was next to him, moving forward, firing, reloading, and firing again, his face grim and determined.

Revenge, thought Gunter. *Revenge for Liesl and Helga.*

The French soldiers were drawing closer now, within reach. A rifle barked and the soldier next to Karl was thrown backwards, arms flying sideways, his rifle dropping to the earth as he collapsed. Gunter broke into a run, rifle and bayonet pointed forwards, a roar rising in his throat, and then he was running and shouting, even though his words couldn't be heard above the rifles, the noise, the screams, the yells.

"Die!" he shouted. "Die!"

He thrust the bayonet forward as a French soldier loomed up in front of him, and felt the blade briefly judder to a stop as it hit the soldier's tunic, and then it tore through the cloth and webbing and sank into the soldier's chest. The soldier screamed, his scream filling Gunter's ears above the noise and chaotic sounds of the battle. Gunter tugged at the rifle to pull the bayonet out, but it snagged on the French soldier's body, and the soldier screamed again in pain. Gunter twisted the bayonet to try and get it loose, then put his boot against the soldier's body and pulled back sharply. This time the bayonet came free. The soldier collapsed, still screaming and writhing in pain.

Gunter stepped over him to confront the next French soldier coming at them, but saw Karl step in front of him and jab with his rifle, the bayonet going into the French soldier's throat.

A rifle went off close to Gunter's head, deafening him. Instinctively, Gunter jerked back and sideways and saw one of his comrades tumble to the ground, shot. Then Gunter swung back, thrusting with his bayonet, and felt it sink into something solid.

Now it was hand-to-hand, soldier against soldier, bayonets, knives, revolvers fired up close, rifles used as clubs, as the French threw themselves against the German defensive line, and the Germans fought back. Soldiers from both sides fell, some dead, most wounded and dying, their cries of agony wailing through the air.

And then, suddenly, it was over. The sound of distant whistles from the French lines, and the French began to withdraw, walking backwards, rifles still firing, but retreating.

A few shots came from the German lines, fired at the retreating soldiers, but four blasts of the whistle brought the firing to an end.

Gunter looked around at his comrades, checking on who was still alive, and was relieved to see Karl standing, clutching his rifle and staring after the retreating French.

He had come through. They had both come through. There would be no more talk of Karl walking home.

There was no feeling of victory in the small cave that night. An attack had been repulsed. The French had withdrawn for the moment. They would be back again the next day. And the day after. And the day after that. In a few days' time, Gunter and his comrades would be given the order to go over the top and they would advance towards the French lines, following on from an initial barrage of their own heavy artillery. But, for the moment, they could sleep this night in their cave and know the enemy had not been able to make any advance. They had held them back.

Gunter sat in the broken armchair and looked at where Karl was sitting on one of the battered chairs made of wooden crates. Like them, their four comrades who were taking refuge in the cave were bunking down for sleep as best they could on the old chairs, one using the table as a bed. Gunter hadn't had a chance to talk to Karl properly after the battle, but then, he wasn't sure it would have been a wise thing to do. Karl had risen to the challenge during the battle. Why bring up the subject of Liesl and Helga and plunge his friend back into misery and self-doubt again?

He looked across at Karl, who was sitting upright in his chair, not relaxing, the expression on his face grim and hard, his eyes open but seeing nothing.

He is looking inward, thought Gunter. *He is still thinking of the bombs falling on our town, and Liesl and Helga dead.*

At the thought of his sister, Gunter bit his lip hard and fought not to let his tears show.

His beloved sister was dead. Tomorrow, and for ever, she would be dead. Never again would he see her face smiling at him, feel her hand in his, hear her laugh.

But tomorrow, I will make them pay for her death, he vowed. *The French and the British.*

He looked again across at Karl, sitting angry and mute, staring at nothing.

Tomorrow, we will talk, he promised. *Together, we will get through this. And when the War is over, we will build our lives anew.*

Gunter woke to the sound of activity from outside the cave. The sound of hammers beating against metal, the grunts and thuds as men put sandbags in place along the top of the trench, all to reinforce the defences.

He sat up from where he lay sprawled in the armchair. As always, his joints and back ached. There was no comfort in sleeping half-upright in a broken armchair. He looked around the cave, and saw that all of his comrades were still asleep, except for Karl. The chair he'd last seen Karl sitting on was empty.

Was Karl out there in the trench with the others, helping to reinforce the defences?

Gunter pushed himself up out of the armchair, grabbed his rifle, helmet and gas mask, and ducked out through the entrance to the cave where all the activity was going on in the trench.

Men were walking along the duckboards, carrying sandbags. Others were cleaning their rifles. There was no sign of Karl.

Perhaps he has gone to the latrines, thought Gunter. Not that there was actually a proper latrine – the men went to a separate area and did their toilet business in a stinking hole that had been marked out away from the trench. Gunter went there now to relieve himself, and also to search for Karl. But Karl wasn't there.

"Have you seen Karl Waldheim?" Gunter asked one of the soldiers carrying sandbags, but the man shook his head. Gunter got the same answer from everyone he asked. No one had seen Karl.

It was another two hours before Gunter found out what had

happened. The news came back from a patrol that had gone out just after dawn to check No Man's Land.

"We found your friend, Karl," said the patrolman. He held out the identity tags and a wallet to Gunter. "We brought these back, in case you wanted to send them back to anyone at home. He had a sweetheart, didn't he?"

Gunter took them, and stared at them, bewildered.

"Yes," he said, numbly. He opened the wallet. It was Karl's, and inside there was a photo of Liesl, and one of Helga with Karl and their mother.

"Where did you find him?" he demanded, his tone one of bafflement. "What happened?"

"It seems he came out into the trench in the early hours of the morning, when it was still dark," replied the patrolman. "He told the sentry on duty that he was going for a walk. The sentry thought he just meant he was getting some fresh air, but then Karl said he was going home. The sentry laughed, thinking Karl was making a joke. And Karl laughed, too, so the sentry was sure he was making a joke.

"A little later, the sentry looked along the line and saw a figure climbing out of the trench, and over the top, and start walking towards No Man's Land. The sentry said he called for the man to stop, but the man kept walking. The sentry was pretty sure it was Karl, but he was some distance away, and it was dark. The sentry didn't know what to do, he didn't know whether to call an officer.

"Then the moon came out from behind a cloud, and the sentry said he saw clearly that it was Karl, and he was holding his revolver ahead of him, aimed towards the enemy lines. And then he said a mist came up, you know: the marsh mist that comes up from the clay, and Karl kept walking, right into the mist, and then he disappeared from sight."

Heinz shook his head sadly.

"They must have seen him coming and shot him," he said. "When we found him, he was riddled with bullets." He looked at Gunter, puzzled. "Why did he do it?" he asked. "Why did he try and launch an attack all on his own? It was stupid!"

"Because he was a brave man," said Gunter.

But inside, his inner voice told him: *Because they were in his way, and Karl was walking home.*

18 October 1916–8 April 1917

The Anglo-French daylight bombing raid on Oberndorf on 12 October killed five civilians and put the rifle factory out of action for two days. Nine bombers were destroyed in the raid by anti-aircraft fire. When the cost of the Allied casualties were set against the result, the factory only shut down for two days, the mission was considered a military failure, and further daylight bombing raids were suspended.

Another casualty of the Oberndorf raid was an American pilot, Norman Prince. Although America had not yet entered the War, Norman Prince had been determined to play his part for the Allies, and he persuaded the French to allow the setting up of the American Escadrille Squadron (a team of American fighter pilots flying under the French flag) in April 1916. Prince took part in 122 aerial combats, including flying as an escort for the bombing raid on Oberndorf. As he returned to his home base his landing wheels hit telegraph cables, his plane turned over, and crashed. He died of his injuries three days later, on 15 October. His body was returned to the United States and given a hero's burial at the National Cathedral in Washington DC.

The Battle of the Somme began on 1 July 1916 and ended on 18 November. It was one of the bloodiest battles in the history of warfare, with over a million men wounded or killed during those four and a half months. Reports of casualty rates for both sides have varied since the battle. One "authoritative source" puts the figures at: 620,000 Allied casualties, and 500,000 from the Central Powers forces, a total of 1,120,000. Another source, claiming to be equally authoritative, puts the figures at: British-French casualties: 947,289; German/Central Powers: 719,000. Total: 1,666,289.

The War on all fronts continued through the winter of 1916/1917 and continued to be a stalemate.

With the coming of spring in 1917, a major new player entered the fray: on 6 April 1917, the United States of America joined the Allies, declaring war on Germany. For some time there had been anger in America at the conduct of Germany during the War, particularly the attacks by German U-boats on shipping, where Americans had lost their lives, as had happened with the sinking of the *Lusitania*. Early in 1917 this situation worsened as German U-boats sank seven US merchant ships they believed were carrying supplies to Europe.

Then the US Intelligence services were passed a telegram sent by the German Foreign Minister to the Mexican Government. In this, the Germans invited Mexico to become their allies in the War. In return, they offered to help Mexico get back the territories of Texas, Arizona and New Mexico that it had lost to America in the Mexican-American War of 1846 to 1848. For the Americans, and for their President, Woodrow Wilson, this was a step too far.

The impact of America entering the War was crucial for the Allies, with 4 million military personnel coming from the States, although the first American troops did not enter the action until late in 1917.

As we have seen, the countries that made up Britain's Empire at this time, including Australia, New Zealand, Canada, India, Ireland, the West Indies, South Africa and Rhodesia (now Zimbabwe) had sent troops to fight alongside the British and the French. Canada had entered the fray alongside Britain from the beginning, in August 1914. Possibly Canada's finest hour in the First World War was during the Battle of Arras in April 1917, when they were given the objective of taking the heavily defended Vimy Ridge.

Vimy Ridge was high ground controlled by the Germans. From their elevated position, the Germans could thwart Allied attacks. If the Allies were going to be able to make any progress forward, the Canadians had to take Vimy Ridge.

Vimy Ridge

9 April 1917

"What are we gonna do?" Carl Wessheim looked up from the letter he was reading and glanced at Arnie, his eldest brother, who was pacing anxiously around the small concrete structure they'd made into their base; part of the network of trenches and tunnels that formed the Allied front line in France. His other brother, Bernie, sat and thought about the problem, just as Carl and Arnie did. Bernie had always been the silent one. Arnie was the one who led and talked, made the decisions. Arnie wasn't just their older brother, he was also a Lieutenant, an officer who gave them their orders. But right now he was anxiously, urgently, asking their advice.

Carl Wessheim was one of eight brothers and sisters: Arnie, who was 29; then came Bernie, 27, then Carl, 25, followed by Delia, 23, Elsie 21, Florence, 20, Henry, 18, and the youngest, Irene, just 13. Carl had often wondered if their parents had been aiming to have 26 children, just to get the whole alphabet in. Carl, Arnie and Bernie had been out here in France with the Canadian Corps for the last three years. The girls were back at home in Toronto with Ma and Pop. The problem the three brothers were discussing right now was their youngest brother, Henry.

Carl read the letter their mother had written to Arnie again.

Dear Arnold,

I am writing to you to beg you to do something to stop Henry joining up and coming out. I know you boys are doing a great job over there, and I worry about you all the time, but I know you are all able to take care of yourselves. I'm afraid for Henry. You know what he's like, he's so headstrong he's likely to get himself killed. The thing is, he looks up to you, and to Bernard and Carl. If you tell him not to go to France, I hope he won't. And if he won't listen to you, could you talk to your commanding officers and get them to turn Henry down? I don't want him going to France. I love you all, but he's my little baby.

Your loving mother

Then Carl turned to the other letter Arnie had given him, which had arrived in the same post. This one was from Henry and was written in the same way that Henry did everything: rushed and scribbled, ink stains and splashes, words started and then crossed out. It was in marked contrast to the neat writing in their mother's letter, as was the sentiment expressed:

Arnie

I know Ma has written to you saying she don't want me to go to France and she wants you to say No to me coming out and joining you. Well, I'm coming out there, and if you stop me joining your outfit

I'm going to join the Royal Flying Corps. They want pilots and there's loads of Canadians going up in planes. So that's what I'm going to do if you try and stop me.

See you soon.

Henry

"The Flying Corps!" groaned Arnie. "Can you imagine Henry in a plane?! He wrecked my bike when he rode it!"

"And mine," nodded Bernie.

And mine, too, remembered Carl ruefully. Even though he'd forbidden Henry to touch it, and had locked it. But somehow Henry had got the lock open and gone off for a spin on it, and crashed it. As Arnie said, the thought of Henry in a plane was too awful to contemplate.

"At least if he's with us, we can keep an eye on him," said Carl.

"How?" demanded Arnie. "We're supposed to be fighting a war! How can we do that properly when we're having to keep one eye on Henry all the time, making sure he doesn't get in trouble? You know what he's like! How many times have we had to get him out of scrapes, at school, in town, everywhere! Look at that time he went to camp and set fire to the tents!"

"It was an accident," said Carl. "The camp leader said it was."

"But it was an accident that happened to *Henry*!" stressed Arnie. "Accidents and disasters happen when he's around! He's like a…"

He stopped, unable to find the right word.

"Jinx?" suggested Bernie.

"Yes, that's it! He's a jinx!" said Arnie. "And if he comes here he'll jinx us! We could lose the War because of him!" His expression became determined as he said: "So I'm going to see Major Sims and tell him not to let Henry come here and join our outfit. Or any other outfit along the line."

"So instead he goes off and joins the Flying Corps?" said Carl.

Arnie fell silent, then he scowled.

"Damn!" he said.

Henry stood and scowled at his three older brothers. He was in uniform, fully trained and armed, and had just arrived in France to join them in the 2nd Canadian Division. He also had a black eye, and this was the topic that had roused Arnie's anger.

"You got in a fight!" said Arnie accusingly.

"It wasn't my fault!" snapped Henry defensively.

"With a fellow soldier!" continued Arnie angrily.

"He started it!" countered Henry.

"How do you make that out!" demanded Arnie. "You threw the first punch! Everyone who saw it said so! You admitted you did!"

"Yes, but…"

"We're supposed to be fighting the Germans!" shouted Arnie.

"And that's how he started it!" shouted back Henry. "He said I was German! Just cos of our name!" He let out a deep and unhappy sigh. "Why didn't Gramps change his name when he came to Canada? Or even Pops!"

"Henry, plenty of people on our side have got German names," Carl pointed out. "Even the King of England has got a German family name. They're called..." He stopped, struggling to remember the British monarchy's family name.

"Saxe-Coburg and Gotha," said Bernie quietly.

"It doesn't matter what our name is," said Arnie. "We're Canadians. That's what we are. And everyone in Canada has come from somewhere else."

"Except the native Indians," said Carl.

Arnie gave him a scowl. "You know what I mean," he said. "*Most* everyone in Canada is from somewhere else. Scotland. Ireland. France. Germany. Holland. Italy. Russia."

"Yeah, but not everyone has got a German name!" retorted Henry.

Arnie shook his head.

"I'm not talking to you any more about this," he declared grimly. "What I am telling you is stay out of trouble. No more fights with our own soldiers."

"But if this guy says—"

"Whatever *anyone* says," stated Arnie firmly. "You keep your fighting for the Germans. And that's an order."

That night, Henry lay in his bunk. He felt angry. He'd volunteered to fight, to play his part in winning this war, and all he'd got was abuse. It had always been the same, right from when they were kids, with either Arnie or Bernie or Carl telling him off. They looked down on him because he was so much younger than him. When he had been six, Arnie had been seventeen, a young man already at work and earning money; and Bernie and Carl hadn't been much better – always moaning at him about something.

Well he was going to show them. He was here now, right in the front line, and he was going to make sure he did something that would make them sit and take notice. Respect him for a soldier, instead of treating him like some kid. He'd show them!

Easter Sunday, 8 April 1917, and Lieutenant Arnold Wessheim addressed his unit. He stood beside a board on which had been chalked a plan of the front line where the two opposing armies faced one another, the crucial point of Vimy Ridge, and the area behind the German lines. All along the Front, every member of the four Divisions of the Canadian Corps was being given the same talk by their officers as preparations for the offensive were co-ordinated.

"Men," announced Arnie, "as you know, for the last two weeks our big guns have been shelling the German positions on Vimy Ridge, and this last week that shelling has been constant. It hasn't just been to wear the Germans down, the shelling has aimed at crushing the barbed wire defences in front of their lines.

"Tomorrow morning, we attack. The plan is to continue with the bombardment on the German positions through the night, and then our guns will stop at just before 0530 hours. They'll be recalibrating the guns ready for a synchronized barrage, which will begin at 0530.

At 0531, engineers will detonate the mines that they've been putting in tunnels they've dug beneath No Man's Land, right up to the German front line.

"The effect should be that the German defences will crumble, or be damaged enough for us to get right through their front line. Once we're through, we keep on going. Our objective is to capture the town of Les Tilleuls and then take the Ridge." And Arnie pointed at the town on his chalked map. "The 1st, 3rd and 4th Divisions will be going into action at the same time, making their assaults on their own areas. We *all* have to succeed, because if only one of our divisions makes it through but the others don't, they'll be exposed to German fire from their flanks. This is a concentrated and co-ordinated action. Get this right, and this could win the Allies the War. Get it wrong, and it won't be just our unit who lose, but all our comrades all along the line.

"As you will have seen, it's sleet and snow out there, and a north-westerly wind. If it stays like that, it'll be blowing snow into the faces of the Germans, which will help us. But we can't depend on the weather. We have to depend on one another. We're brothers in arms. Remember that.

"OK. Take your positions in the forward trenches. Make sure everything's working, we don't want any guns jamming. And may God be with us."

With that, he gestured for the unit to head for their positions, then he pointed at Henry.

"Private Henry Wessheim, you're with me."

Frowning, Henry came over to Arnie.

"What's up, Arnie?" he asked.

Arnie scowled.

"You address me as Lieutenant or sir. Got that?"

Henry hesitated, then said, "Yes, sir."

"Right. When the attack starts, you stay close to me. Right."

"Why?" demanded Henry. Adding, quickly: "Sir?"

"Because I'm your superior officer and I said so," said Arnie. "From here on in, you stay right by me, where I can see you."

Henry glared at Arnie, and Arnie could almost see the phrase "Stop treating me like a little kid!" about to burst out angrily from Henry's mouth. Instead, Henry took a deep breath, then asked: "Will it be all right if I go to the latrines? Sir!"

Arnie glowered at his youngest brother, but then nodded.

"Very well, Private. But report back to me immediately after."

After Henry had left, Bernie and Carl joined Arnie.

"You can't protect him during the battle," said Carl. "We have to let him grow up."

"That's what I want him to do," snapped back Arnie. "I don't want him running off and doing some fool thing that gets him killed. I promised Ma I'd take care of him, and that's what I'm doing."

"It ain't fair on him, Arnie," said Bernie quietly. "You're gonna make him look bad in front of the other guys if you wrap him up in cotton wool."

"He's our little brother," replied Arnie fiercely. "And I ain't wrapping him up. He's gonna be in that battle, same as us, same as every man here. I just wanna keep an eye on him, like I promised Ma."

"And if you get yourself killed?" pushed Carl. "Because you're not paying proper attention to what you should be doing?"

Arnie shook his head.

"I can take care of myself," he said. He saw Henry returning. "OK," he said. "Let's go get ourselves in position."

Henry stood in line in the trench along with the other soldiers, rifle ready. The wooden scaling ladders were in place against the wall of the trench. From behind came the continuous rumble and deafening explosions of the Allied heavy guns as they continued their battering of the German lines, as they had done constantly for the past two weeks. Or so Henry had been told. He'd been out here just three days and was eager for action. So far all he'd done was wait and listen to the big guns and the returning fire from the Germans. He wanted to *be* there. To get out there and fight the enemy, man-to-man, face-to-face.

Arnie, Bernie and Carl had been doing that for almost three years now, and they were still alive, despite the scare stories his ma had told him about men dying by the thousands to try to put him off from joining up.

The snow and sleet swirled around them as they waited and his face and fingers felt cold, even with the fingerless mittens he wore and the woollen balaclava helmet.

He looked at Arnie standing next to him, his brother's attention turned on the top of the trench, his whistle between his lips, ready to blow for the attack.

Suddenly, the shelling from the big guns behind them stopped.

A few seconds, Arnie had said. To recalibrate the guns so they could get ready for a synchronized barrage.

The sudden silence was stunning after hours and hours of constant ear-splitting mind-numbing noise.

Henry counted the seconds. One, two, three, four, five, six, seven… He got to thirty, and then the guns opened up again, their target now the German defences further in.

Simultaneously there was a massive explosion from the other side of No Man's Land that shook the ground around them as the mines that had been laid beneath the German front lines were detonated. The explosion was so huge that Henry thought the trench might collapse on them, burying them.

He looked along the line of men, all standing as he was, rifle ready, tin hat on. Carl and Bernie were just along the line from him. Were they under orders from Arnie to stay close to him? To look after their kid brother? Well if that was their plan, they were mistaken. He was a soldier, just like they were, and he was going to make them proud of him.

The barrage continued, heavy shells and firing from the field guns. The ground around him was still shaking from the explosion of the mines.

PEEEEEP! The shrill blast of Arnie's whistle could be heard, even with the sound of the guns, and Henry leapt forward, grabbing one of the rungs of the ladder with one hand, and hauled himself up, the men on either side of him doing the same. He thought he heard Arnie's voice shout "Wait!" at him, but he wasn't going to wait. He was going into action. This was his moment!

Carl scaled the ladder and heaved himself over the edge of the trench, Bernie alongside him. Ahead of them were the hunched backs of their comrades, advancing towards the German lines, hurrying, taking advantage of the lull in the firing as a result of the underground mines being detonated. The barrage from behind them continued, shells raining down on the Germans' position. The snow and sleet swirled around him, making visibility difficult. He couldn't make out who was who, it was just a mass of men in mist and snow moving forward. He followed, rifle pointing forward, finger on the trigger.

Beneath his boots the ground was uneven, deep pits and rifts from shells and weather. He couldn't see Arnie, or Henry, and he suddenly realized that Bernie had disappeared from beside him.

There was firing now coming from ahead, and bullets struck the ground around him. The Germans had recovered sufficiently to begin to defend themselves against the offensive, but the barrage increased and the firing died a little. But not completely. The man directly in front of Carl suddenly collapsed, and Carl stumbled as he tried to avoid treading on him, that stumble saving his life as a hail of bullets struck the ground where he'd been standing a second before.

Carl pushed on, firing into the snow-filled mass ahead of him, sliding the bolt to eject the empty shell and put another bullet in the breech. The sound around him was now deafening, all-encompassing: the big guns and their heavy barrage, the field guns, howitzers, incoming rifle fire and the ratatatatat of machine guns; howls of pain around him; and he moved on, running now, crouching low, although he knew that wouldn't help if a bullet took him in the legs or the chest. He ran over half-buried barbed wire, the sharp tangles picking at his legs, tearing at the thick bandage-like material the soldiers wore around their lower legs.

And then, suddenly, the first German trench was in view, and as he fired towards it, he recognized Bernie running past him, firing, and he joined him, caught up with him, and together they ran, shooting and reloading, shooting and reloading…

Some of the German soldiers were scrambling out of the trench and coming towards them, rifles raised. Explosions echoed, rifles being fired up close, and the soldiers in front of them toppled and then fell, some face forward, some tumbling backwards into the trench.

Onward they ran, Carl and Bernie, the rifles hot in their hands, and then they were sliding down into the German trench, landing on bodies and parts of bodies.

Arnie scoured the scene ahead and around him: the bodies of his comrades lying half-in and out of water-filled mud-holes. The sound of firing through the cloud of snow and sleet told him the attack was still progressing, but where was Henry?

That damn stupid kid! he thought angrily, his heart full of pain at the thought that one of the bodies lying on the ground could well be Henry's. *His first action, and he dies!* Tears welled up in Arnie's eyes, and he was filled with dread at the thought of how he was going to tell their mother the news.

But he was a Lieutenant, a leader, and the attack must succeed! He turned to resume his advance with his comrades towards the German lines, and as he did he felt a tearing pain in his chest as a bullet tore into him, and then he was falling…

Carl and Bernie stood surveying the wreckage of the town of Les Tilleuls. They'd made it; they'd reached their objective. Around them, Canadian soldiers were mopping up, taking prisoners, checking for booby traps.

Bernie turned and looked back the way they'd come, across a sea of mud and bodies on which snow was beginning to settle.

"Any sign of them?" asked Carl.

Bernie shook his head.

"Think they made it?" asked Carl, and this time his tone was more hesitant.

Bernie was silent.

"We ought to go back and look," said Carl.

"The Lieutenant said we had to move forward," replied Bernie. "We've got to take the rest of the Ridge. We've got to consolidate the position."

"Yes, but—" Carl began to argue.

Bernie shook his head.

"Orders are orders," he said simply. He gestured to where the other soldiers were already moving onward, fanning out, securing the high ground. "Arnie told us what we had to do."

It was only after the Ridge had been secured that Carl was able to get Bernie to agree to let him backtrack and search for Arnie and Henry. Officially, if stopped, he would tell other soldiers in their positions that he had a message to deliver to Lieutenant Wessheim, and ask if they knew where he was; but each time his quest was met with a shake of a head, and a suggestion he try further down the line.

It was a near impossible task. One hundred and seventy thousand men had taken part in the attack and hundreds and hundreds of bodies littered the ground, still being picked up by medical orderlies. Trying to find Arnie and Henry among them was like trying to find a needle in a haystack. It was worse, it was like trying to find a particular blade of hay in a haystack. But Carl knew he had to try. If his brothers were dead, then their parents had to be told.

He came across a small group of soldiers from his own Division who were making camp in what had been a German defence post.

"Hi, guys," he greeted them. "I'm trying to find Lieutenant Wessheim. Have you seen him?"

"He got shot," replied one of the soldiers.

Shot! Carl did his best not to let his feelings show as he asked: "Wh-Where was he?"

The soldier gestured along the line of bodies.

"Back there," said the soldier. "He was lucky. Some kid came and picked him up and carried him to safety, and then he carried on rushing at the Germans." He shook his head. "He'd only just come out here as well. Crazy kid!" Then the soldier caught sight of someone approaching because he grinned and said: "And here he is!"

Carl turned and saw Henry approaching, rifle slung over his shoulder.

"Hey, Carl!" called Henry, smiling broadly. "You're alive!"

Carl nodded.

"I hear you saved Arnie," he said.

Henry gave a self-conscious grin and a shrug.

"Someone had to," he said. "Ma would never have forgiven me if I didn't. Where's Bernie?"

Carl pointed along the route he'd just walked.

"Up on the Ridge," he said.

"Guess I'd better go and make sure he's OK," said Henry. "Lucky I'm here to take care of you guys!"

With that, Henry began to walk along the rutted track towards the Ridge.

"Good kid," said the soldier.

"Yes," nodded Carl. "He is."

13 April–1 June 1917

The Battle of Vimy Ridge was the first time that all four divisions of the Canadian Corps took part in a battle together. The attack began at 0530 on 9 April, and by 0700 the 1st, 2nd and 3rd Divisions had reached their first objectives, and the 2nd Division had taken the town of Les Tilleuls. By nightfall on 12 April 1917, the Canadians had taken control of the Ridge, with losses of 3,600 dead and 7,000 wounded. The German casualty figures are unknown, although about 4,000 were taken prisoner.

Four members of the Canadian Corps received the Victoria Cross for their actions during the battle: Pte William Mile, Pte John Pattison, Lance-Sgt Ellis Sifton, and Capt Thain MacDowell.

A 250-acre memorial stands at Vimy Ridge, dedicated to the battle, and to the Canadian soldiers who died.

Despite the success of the Canadians at Vimy Ridge, and that of British and Australian forces elsewhere at the Battle of Arras, by mid-summer it was obvious that once again the battle in France had reached a stalemate, with neither side making any major victories, or gaining ground.

The possibility of a continuing – almost endless – stalemate had occupied the Allies for some time, and it was British General Plumer who came up with the idea of digging tunnels deep beneath the German lines at Messines and filling them with explosives. Not just a few tons of explosives, but many hundreds. These would be known as the Mines of Messines.

The Mines of Messines

2 June 1917

BOOOOOM!!! The earth beneath their feet, and the walls and roof of the tunnel shook as the bombs struck.

Deep beneath the surface, seventeen-year-old Jim Smith stopped hacking at the wall with his pickaxe, as did his dad, his Uncle Ned, and the hundreds of other men at work. Apprehensively, the men looked up at the roof. Even though it was shored up with wooden struts there was always the fear that the wooden supports would work loose, shaken by the bombing, or by the movement of the earth itself. If that happened, then thousands of tons of clay could come down on them.

More bombs fell on the ground above, shaking the earth, but the tunnel held.

"That was close!" said the young man next to Jim nervously. He'd only come out to France the day before.

"You get used to it," shrugged Jim.

The young man shook his head.

"I don't think I'll ever get used to this," he said. "I mean, things were hard back home, but at least we didn't have people trying to kill us."

"Where you from?" asked Jim.

"Yorkshire," he replied. "I'm a coal miner. My name's Bob McVay."

"Jim Smith," said Jim, and the two men shook hands.

"You been out here long?" asked Bob.

"Since February," said Jim. "Just over three months."

"You've been lucky!" said Bob.

"Lucky?" echoed Jim, puzzled.

"To still be alive," said Bob. "I hear that men are dying by the hundreds out here."

"Mainly soldiers," nodded Jim. "We're the lucky ones. We're not out in the open getting shot at."

"Unless a bomb brings that roof down."

"Don't think about it," said Jim. "Think about it and it'll happen. That's what they say here."

"I was supposed to be getting married next week," said Bob ruefully. "We'd booked the church and everything, and then I got called up to come out here."

"She'll still be there when you get back," said Jim.

"Will she, though?" asked Bob uncertainly. "Her mum doesn't like me. She wanted Lettie to marry some posh bloke with money. Now I'm out of the way..."

"OK, lads!" called Jim's dad. "Break over! Let's get back to work."

Along with the others, Jim and Bob returned to their tasks, hacking at the clay, digging further into the mass of earth, then shovelling it into the waiting wheelbarrow.

It was a long and slow job, because everything had to be done by hand: the digging and the wheeling of the barrows with the clay to the tunnel entrance. If any machines were used, the Germans might pick up their sound and realize what was going on deep beneath their feet, and these tunnels were meant to be top secret.

Work on them had been going on since February 1917. Months of hard digging in heavy clay by hundreds and hundreds of men, an army of navvies. Jim had been working as a navvy, a tunnel digger, since he was fourteen. He dug because that was what all the men in his family had ever done. He'd joined Dad and Uncle Ned digging the tunnels for London's underground railway and sewers as soon as he left school. His grandfather had also dug London's tunnels. His *great-grandfather* had dug London's canals. Being a navvy was in Jim's family.

When the War began, Jim's dad and his Uncle Ned had volunteered to join the Army and fight, but the Government had told them that the work they did, digging London's tunnels, was much more important, so they'd stayed in England. Now, the Government needed the navvies in France, on the battlefields of the Somme. Or, rather, beneath the battlefields at a place called Messines.

The War on the Western Front had been at a stalemate for nearly three years, with neither side gaining any ground. Despite all the attacks the Allies had launched, the German defences had stood firm. There seemed to be no way through them or past them. Then someone had come up with a radical idea: to dig a series of tunnels beneath the German lines and fill them with explosives. Six hundred tons of explosives, packed into twenty tunnels right beneath the German front line. The theory was that when the explosion went off it would be so devastating that not only would it kill the Germans in their trenches at the front line directly above it, it would send shock waves throughout the whole German defences, collapsing their trenches, stunning their soldiers, and allowing the Allies to launch a major attack through the shattered German front line.

These Mines of Messines were intended to break the stalemate and end this war.

As well as Jim and his dad and his uncle, and hundreds of other men from London, there were coal miners from Yorkshire, like Bob, as well as from Derbyshire, Wales and Scotland, everywhere where navvies and miners worked. All of them were men used to working deep below ground and digging with picks and shovels.

As Jim used his pick to pull the clay out of the walls of the tunnel, he thought about what was happening far above them. Life working in the tunnels was dangerous with the constant threat of a roof collapse or a cave-in, but from what he'd seen, life for the soldiers in the trenches was worse.

The navvies had made a camp for themselves just inside the mouth of the tunnel, which meant they had a roof over their head when it rained. And it rained a lot on the Somme.

The soldiers in the trenches weren't so lucky, they spent their lives in deep puddles of water. Although they had wooden duckboards to walk on, it seemed that often these duckboards sank into the mud and disappeared. When that happened, the soldiers had to wade, sometimes thigh-deep, through muddy water.

When the German shells struck near the trenches, the sides of the trenches often collapsed, and the soldiers had to dig themselves out while the Germans shot at them. Many of the soldiers became sick; not just from the dreadful conditions in the trenches, but also from the rats, which spread diseases.

Jim knew that many soldiers were jealous of the diggers. Not because the navvies were below ground, but because they got paid a lot more. The soldiers were paid a shilling a day, while the navvies received six shillings a day. Jim's dad had nearly got into a fight with a soldier about this. The soldier had said that Jim's dad should pay some of their wages to the soldiers because it was the soldiers who were doing the fighting. Jim's dad pointed out that the diggers hadn't asked to be paid more, and he added that if the bombs in these tunnels worked it would put an end to the War and they could all go home. But the tunnels couldn't be dug by ordinary soldiers, they had to be dug by experts who knew what they were doing. The diggers.

Fortunately, an officer had come along and stopped the argument before it turned into a fight. But there was still that resentment among some of the soldiers.

Not all, though. Most of the soldiers in the trenches seemed to be aware of the importance of the digging that was going on, and urged Jim and his pals to "dig faster". But that wasn't the proper way to dig a tunnel that would last. It had to be done slowly and methodically: dig into the clay, then put the wooden posts in place to support the roof and walls before moving on to dig out the next section. And the posts needed to be put in place without too much hammering for fear of alerting the Germans. Nothing was simple about these tunnels.

Finally, after hours of endless and back-breaking work, a whistle blew to announce the shift change-over; and Jim and the other men took their tools back to their camp at the tunnel entrance, while the next shift arrived to take their places. Digging these tunnels was a 24-hour-a-day operation.

A brazier made from an old tin drum, heaped with coals, was burning in their makeshift camp. It kept them warm, but more importantly, it kept the kettles boiling for mugs of tea. The mugs, like the kettles, had turned black from the smoke from the brazier, but to Jim the dirt didn't matter. There was no way you could be fussy about dirt out here: muck and mud were all around you. You lived with it.

Jim settled himself down on an old wooden crate with his mug of thick tea, sweetened with condensed milk. There was no fresh milk or sugar out here. He'd heard that further along the line, a bunch of navvies had found a cow wandering, strayed from the remains of a destroyed farm, and had brought it into their camp so they could have fresh milk. Personally, Jim doubted if the story was true. People made stories like that up to try and make life more interesting. The ones about the rats here being as big as cats were true, though. He'd seen them: great fat hairy animals with long tails and vicious-looking teeth.

He gestured for the new man, Bob, to join him.

Bob pointed towards a crate nearer to the brazier.

"It'll be warmer there," he said. "This place is damp and wet."

"Pecking order," explained Jim. "The seats nearer the fire are for the older blokes and those who've been here longest. You have to earn your place there."

"But you've been here a long time," countered Bob. "You could sit there."

"Yeah, but then I'd be with the old geezers," replied Jim. "I like being with blokes of my own age. Dad and Uncle Ned are all right, but they like to talk about the old times, and I don't remember them."

Bob sipped his tea and nodded.

"It's the same in the mine at home," he said. "All the old gaffers talking about how hard times used to be, like they ain't now." He shook his head. "I'm gonna leave the mine when I get home."

"And do what?" asked Jim.

Bob shrugged.

"I dunno," he said. "Something where I don't spend my life underground the whole time. Maybe join a fair or a travelling circus."

"A circus!" exclaimed Jim, stunned.

"It's a good life," said Bob. "You get to travel and meet people."

"What would you do in a circus?"

"Put up the big tent," said Bob. "There's always work for a strong bloke in a circus."

"Have you told your fiancée?" asked Jim. "About joining the circus."

"Lettie," said Bob. "Not yet," he admitted. "She'd tell her mum, and her mum would stop us getting married. She thinks me being a miner is low. If she thought I was working in a circus, that'd be even worse."

"And if you were travelling around all over the place, you wouldn't see much of your missus."

"She could join me," said Bob. Then he added doubtfully: "Though I can't see her being happy living in a caravan. She wants a proper house. At least, her mum does." He gave a rueful sigh. "Her mum says she's coming to live with us when we're married."

Jim sighed.

"Good luck with that!" he said sympathetically.

The next day, Jim and his gang were back on their shift, digging and hauling, driving the tunnel further along. From the measurements the engineers had made, it was reckoned they were now well beneath the German front line.

"Not much longer now, son," Jim's dad said, as they lifted the handles of their wheelbarrows and began to wheel their loads of clay over the wooden boards of the floor of the tunnel. Jim was in the lead, a line of men including his dad and Bob behind him following, pushing their barrows. Suddenly there was an ear-splitting explosion above them and the roof began to cave in.

Instinctively, Jim dropped his barrow and threw himself forward, scrambling for the entrance; then he stopped himself and turned back, desperate to see if his dad was all right.

All he could see was a mass of clay, a whole new wall of earth appearing where a few seconds before had been tunnel and men.

Frantically, Jim grabbed a spade and began digging, hurling the thick wet clay aside. Other men had run in from outside with their spades and pickaxes and joined him.

The cave-in had collapsed the wooden spars that held up the roof, and now they were lodged among the clay. Desperately, other men carried in posts and began to hammer them in place as Jim and others dug furiously. Then Jim threw his spade aside and began to claw at the clay with his bare hands, terrified that the blade of his spade might cut through the clay and hit his dad, or one of the other men. The effect would be the same as a sharp bayonet.

They dug and clawed, but the cave-in had been massive, tons and tons of earth. *Maybe Dad had found an air pocket,* Jim prayed as he tore at the earth. *Maybe the wooden posts had fallen in such a way that they'd formed some kind of protection against the collapsing earth, making a kind of bubble. Maybe the wheelbarrow had turned upside down in the fall and Dad had managed to crawl inside it?*

"Dad!" Jim called as he dug, hoping to hear an answering response; but there was none.

The clay is too thick, reasoned Jim. *He can't hear me because it's too thick and solid. It's like soundproofing.*

Suddenly, a hole was punched in the clay from the other side of the cave-in, and for a second Jim's heart leapt with relief. His dad had escaped!

But it was Uncle Ned, shovel in hand, who'd been digging his way out from the other side of the cave-in.

Grimly, Uncle Ned attacked the mass of clay, digging and hacking at it, clearing.

"Careful!" warned Jim. "You might hit them!"

"If we don't get to them, they'll suffocate!" snapped back Ned. "This is clay! No air in clay!"

They dug, all the men desperately tearing at the fallen clay and hurling it aside. Jim didn't know how long had passed. Five minutes? Ten? Longer?

Suddenly he uncovered the toe of a boot.

"Someone's here!" he yelled.

Taking more care now, they all dug, pulling the clay off, revealing more of the boot, then the leg. Who was it? And why weren't they moving?

More and more clay was cleared away. The legs were now fully exposed, then the belt buckle, then a hand. Still no movement. The chest was exposed, a shirt, with a pattern on. It wasn't his dad, thought Jim with relief. That wasn't his shirt.

Finally, the earth was clawed away from the neck and head.

It was Bob, the young coal miner from Yorkshire, and he wouldn't be going to join any circus. He was dead.

"Another one here!" called a voice.

Jim hurried to join in, still desperately hoping that this one would be his dad, maybe hurt, but still alive. He reached them as Uncle Ned was pulling the limp body out from beneath the mass of fallen earth. The man had got tangled up with the wooden wheelbarrow, which made pulling him out harder.

Uncle Ned turned the body over and cleared the clay from the face.

It was Jim's dad. Like Bob, he was dead. Clay was in his ears and his mouth and his nostrils.

"He'd have died quick," commented one man, trying to make it seem better.

It didn't, not to Jim. It wouldn't have been quick. His dad would have died desperate to breathe, but with his hands and arms trapped by the fall, he wouldn't have been able to attempt to clear the heavy earth. He wouldn't even have been able to move. He'd just have had to lie there, choking, knowing that he was dying and there was nothing anyone could do to save him.

As well as his dad and Bob, ten other men had been killed by the tunnel cave-in. After the bodies had been taken away, Jim and Uncle Ned sat outside the entrance to the tunnel. Jim knew that they should have been back inside the tunnel, helping to clear the rest of the cave-in and shore the roof and walls up again; but the officer in charge had told them to take ten minutes.

Ten minutes! thought Jim bitterly. *Ten minutes for a lifetime!*

"I want to fight," he announced fiercely. "I don't want to just dig tunnels. I want to be out there, with a rifle, killing the Hun. That's what I should be doing!"

Uncle Ned shook his head.

"Each to his own, Jim," he said. "Don't forget, your dad was my brother. I knew him for a lot longer than you did, and I'm as hurt as you. But it won't help you going out there and getting killed as well. The way to pay them back is for us to finish this tunnel, and then blow them sky high." He patted Jim on the shoulder. "Come on," he said. "We can shed tears later, when the job's done."

As they stood up, Jim said helplessly: "What am I going to say to Mum?"

"Tell her the truth," said Ned. "He died for his country; and when we win, it'll be thanks to him and the others that died."

Jim shook his head.

"It won't make it any better," he said. "He's dead."

"True," said Ned. "But he died for something he believed in."

For the next few days, Jim worked harder than he'd worked before, even taking on extra shifts. It was as if he was driven and he was putting every second of his life in to getting this tunnel finished. The other men seemed to be working at the same feverish pace, as if aware that it only needed one last surge to get the tunnels into action. Finally, the engineers declared the tunnel was ready; and so were the other eighteen. Apparently, one of the tunnels had collapsed completely, and rather than lose precious time in re-digging it, it had been decided to go ahead with nineteen tunnels.

When it was announced that the tunnel-digging was complete, Jim, Uncle Ned and the other diggers spent that last day walking along their tunnel, checking that the wooden timbers holding up the roof were strong enough to support the clay.

"We're going to need you to stay around while we put the explosives in, just in case any part of the tunnel collapses," the Captain in charge told them, joining them for this last inspection.

Jim nodded. With the German shells still falling, anything could go wrong.

The diggers took positions along the tunnels with their picks and shovels, and watched as the soldiers carried in wooden boxes containing explosives. Very carefully, the soldiers stacked the boxes at the far end of the tunnels, then went out and returned with more boxes. By the time they'd finished, the tunnel was filled with hundreds of boxes of explosives.

After them came the engineers with coils of copper wire. They fixed detonators to the boxes, and attached the ends of the copper wires to the detonators, then unrolled the coils of copper wire to the entrance to the tunnels.

All the time the shelling from the Germans continued overhead, and the tunnel shook with each new blast. Jim felt nervous as he watched the sides of the tunnels shake, and the roof move slightly. If that lot came down on the explosives it could well trigger the detonators and set them off, and if that happened, then Jim and everyone around would be blown to pieces. But so far the timbers holding up the roof and keeping the sides held firm.

When the last of the copper wires had been unrolled, the Captain nodded at the diggers.

"OK," said the Captain. "Time for you lot to get clear."

As Jim and the rest of the diggers came out of the tunnel, Uncle Ned asked: "What's the time, Jim?"

Jim looked at his watch.

"Two o' clock," he said.

Above them the night sky was lit up with explosions and tracers of bullets from the German lines.

The troops had already withdrawn to a position a few miles away from the tunnels. Jim and the other diggers joined the engineers as they headed for the same position.

Some engineers were unrolling more coils of copper wire. They'd fixed the ends to the wires at the end of the tunnel and were hauling them further away, to where the troops were waiting.

As Jim drew near the troops he saw that they were all in full battle-dress with their metal helmets on and their rifles ready.

"What happens now?" he asked Uncle Ned.

"Now, we hope all those explosives go off," replied Ned. "Because once they do, our big guns open up and shell the Germans. And then those troops launch an attack. If the explosives all go off then the Germans won't know what's happening and we'll win. Trouble is, if only some of the explosives go off, then the Germans who are left will pick them off like flies with their machine guns and they'll die. And all that work will have been for nothing."

Jim looked towards where the engineers were fixing the end of the copper wire to detonator boxes. When the handles on the boxes were turned it would set off the charges deep in the tunnels.

"Right, men!" called the Captain, addressing the massed ranks of soldiers, engineers and diggers. "In a few moments the explosive charges will go off. This will be the biggest explosion the world has ever known. I advise you to be prepared. It should only affect the Germans, but it could send shock waves as far as here."

The Captain checked his watch. He looked towards the place where the engineers were waiting to turn the handles that would set off the explosives. He raised his hand.

"On my mark!" he called. "Five. Four. Three. Two. One. Fire!"

Jim didn't remember much about what happened next. He was deafened by the loudest sound he'd ever heard, and a massive column of fire shot out through the ground in front of him and went up into the night sky. At the same time the earth beneath his feet lifted up and he was thrown to the ground, as were many of the other men standing with him.

The whole night sky was lit up by explosives and shells as if it was daylight. He felt the vibration of the big guns going off behind the Allied front line, shelling the German positions. The soldiers near him began to run towards the barbed wire of No Man's Land and the German lines beyond.

At that moment his ears popped and his hearing returned. The sound was incredible. Big guns and rifles firing. Men shouting.

He was aware of something heading towards him, and then something hard struck him full in the face, and everything went black.

When he came round he was in a bed with a nurse bending over him.

"Where am I?" he asked.

"You're in hospital," she said. "You got hit in the face by a rock and knocked out. They thought you were dead. You've been unconscious for nearly a day."

"What happened in the attack?" asked Jim. "Did it work?"

The nurse shook her head.

"I'm not allowed to talk about things like that," she said. "I'll come back and check on you later."

With that she left. Jim scowled. He felt frustrated. He wanted to know what had happened.

"You're awake!" said Uncle Ned's voice, relieved.

Jim turned his head and saw his uncle had arrived beside his bed.

"The nurse said you'd come round," he said. "You had me worried for a while."

"Did the explosions work?"

Ned nodded, and gave a big smile.

"They say the shock of the explosion killed ten thousand German soldiers in one go! Blew the lot of them to smithereens! It was so loud they even heard it and felt it in London. Even the Prime Minister heard it in Downing Street!

"They reckon eighty thousand men took part in the attack afterwards and they captured another five thousand Germans, and pushed three miles behind the German lines. Trust me, Jim, this is it! We've done it! This'll mean the end to this rotten war!"

3 June 1917–April 1918

When the Mines of Messines were set off at 3.10 a.m. on 2 June 1917, the explosion was so huge that it was heard hundreds of miles away, including London. It is estimated that 10,000 men in the German front line died instantly. Immediately following the explosions, nine British and French infantry divisions advanced beneath a continuing barrage from Allied shelling. By 14 June, the entire Messines area had been taken by Allied troops.

Away from the Western Front the War spread: in July 1917, Siam (later known as Thailand) declared war on the Central Powers, as did China in August. In August, Liberia declared war on Germany, and Brazil made its own declaration of war against Germany in October.

Also in July, Lieutenant T E Lawrence, later called Lawrence of Arabia, along with Auda ibu Tayi, a Bedouin tribal leader, led a successful attack by Arab forces on the Turkish-held Jordanian port of Aqaba. This success cemented a relationship Lawrence had forged with the leaders of the Arab tribes since his arrival in the Middle East in 1916.

One interesting event occurred during this time: as a reaction to anti-German feelings in Britain, in July 1917 Britain's King George V issued a royal proclamation changing the name of the British royal family from its Germanic "Saxe-Coburg and Gotha" to "The House of Windsor".

By mid to late 1917, the conflict really could be described as global, with the Battle of Mahiwa in East Africa during October 1917. In Palestine the Turkish Army attacked the Arab Army at Petra, while also in Palestine there was a British victory at Beersheba-Gaza.

On the Western Front, the battles continued. After the initial Allied success at Messines, advances by both sides stalled once more. And not just in the ground war, the skies above the Western Front were another battlefield.

When the First World War began in 1914, aeroplanes were still a relatively recent invention. The first-ever flight in a heavier-than-air machine was by the brothers Orville and Wilbur Wright of the USA in 1903. The first cross-Channel flight from Calais to Dover was made six years later by Louis Blériot in 1909, just five years before the War started.

When the War began in 1914, flying was still in its infancy, but young men flocked to volunteer for the newly formed Royal Flying Corps and Royal Navy Air Service. And not just from Britain, but from Canada and America.

Many of the first planes were unreliable and as dangerous to the men who flew them as they were to the enemy. Flimsily constructed of wood and cloth and wire rigging, often they did not have the strength to hold together under the stresses of flying. Fabric could be stripped from the wing during a long dive; undercarriages would break off during landing. Many pilots died in training – before they ever got to meet the enemy.

Once they got to the battlefields of France and Belgium, the dangers for these young men increased. The life of a fighter pilot with the RFC and the RNAS was a short one, with the average lifespan being two weeks.

On 1 April 1918, the RFC and RNAS were merged to create the Royal Air Force.

At this time the most dominant force in the skies over the Western Front were the German Jastas, the specialized aerial fighting squadrons. And the most famous of these was Jasta 11, led by Manfred von Richthofen, also known as the Red Baron from the distinctive red colour of his fighter plane.

The Red Baron

21 April 1918

The sky was a pale grey streaked with yellow, the first hints of dawn as eighteen-year-old Archie Merton and his three fellow fighter pilots took off: Buster Barnes, Derek Kopp and Wilson Williams. Their mission: to protect a two-seater observation flight.

They were to fly due west to the front line where the Allied trenches ended, cross it, and then turn left and fly north for ten miles, weaving backwards and forwards all the time to enable the observation plane to take photographs of the German defences. Then turn back and head for home.

As they crossed over the front line, anti-aircraft fire began to open up from the Germans. At first they kept to a height of 10,000 feet to lessen the chances of being hit, but the observation plane decided it needed to go down lower to get better photographs, so the four planes followed, keeping their eyes peeled all the time for any attacking enemy aircraft, as well as doing their best to dodge debris and missile fragments from the shells exploding around them in the sky.

They were about halfway through their mission, when Archie was aware of Buster suddenly breaking away from the formation and dropping down to a lower altitude, indicating he must have spotted incoming Germans. Immediately Archie turned his plane in the same direction and followed him. There they were, a formation of six German planes, flying out of the rising sun.

Out of the corner of his eye Archie saw the observation plane continue its flight north. Although common sense should have told them to head back across to British territory, Archie assumed they hadn't achieved as much on this mission as they wanted to. He saw the rear observer working at the big wooden box camera at the side of their plane, and then he turned his attention back to the oncoming German fighter planes.

They were nearly on them now. Buster had already flown one pass, coming at the Germans from below, his guns firing, but the German planes banked and turned and twisted in the air, and his tracer of bullets went past them.

Wilson joined Archie and they hurtled forward after Buster, leaving Derek to circle round and round the observation plane, protecting it as it continued the northward journey, the camera clicking and the heavy photographic plates being changed all the time, despite the hail of gunfire around it.

Archie picked out one of the German planes nearest to him and headed straight for it, coming in from the side, guns firing just ahead of him to hit him in the engine at the front of his plane as he flew forwards.

The Hun had seen him coming because he dropped into a steep

dive to get out of the way of Archie's bullets, and then turned up again sharply. Archie followed him, first down, then up, keeping a watch in all other directions as best as he could, ready to be attacked by one of the rest of the enemy squadron.

The German was good. He ducked and dived in the air, and then circled fast, and suddenly he was coming straight at Archie from his right-hand side, his guns chatter-chatter-chattering. Archie throttled back at the apex of the turn, allowing his plane to side-slip for just a few seconds, long enough to take him out of the German's gunsights so he could put it into a dive.

Down Archie went, then banked into a turn, coming up beneath his German opponent. The German tried to turn sharply, too, but the movement was too fast for him and his plane juddered. It was only for a second, but it was all Archie needed. As the German recovered and began to turn away, Archie let him have a burst of gunfire straight into the back of his plane, tearing his tail to shreds.

Without controls, the German's plane gave a sickening lurch, and then plummeted out of the sky, heading towards the ground 10,000 feet below.

Meanwhile the rest of the air battle was continuing. Buster was still active, zooming in and out between the enemy aircraft, guns firing all the time. Wilson was also in the thick of it. It was madness up there, planes hurtling left and right, looping and turning, tracers of gunfire tearing through the sky.

Suddenly Archie saw another two German planes had entered the fray, and with a shock he saw that one of them was painted bright red instead of the regular dull brown colour, and he realized that he was about to go into combat against none other than the famous Red Baron himself, Baron von Richthofen!

This was an opportunity he'd been waiting for ever since he'd enlisted. To bring down the most famous German fighter pilot! He didn't hesitate. He headed towards the Red Baron's plane, guns blazing, but von Richthofen banked sharply and Archie's line of tracer missed. In fact, von Richthofen had banked so sharply that Archie was sure he'd gone into the turn too fast and was going to go into a spin, but, to his shock, the Red Baron continued the sharp turn, doubling back on himself, and then he was suddenly on Archie's right, and the next second there was a RAT-A-TAT of exploding gunfire and Archie's engine cut out, the propeller juddering to a halt. The Red Baron had shot clean through his engine.

Archie's plane began to fall out of the sky, and he went into reflex action: remembering what to do the many times he'd practised "what to do in the event of engine failure". Only this was more than just a failed engine, this was a dead engine and he was in a machine that was suddenly heavier than air. He was now fighting a losing battle against gravity. And then an even bigger horror struck him as he began to feel a stinging wetness on his clothes and face. The Red Baron's bullets had cut through his fuel line and he was being sprayed with gasoline. It was every pilot's nightmare, to be trapped in a burning plane.

First rule: Don't panic.

Second rule: Put the nose of the plane down and use air currents to keep the plane as level as possible while gravity takes hold. Which meant, keep going forward. But in the sudden movement of action, Archie had lost his sense of direction and didn't know whether he was heading towards his own lines, or the German positions.

Third rule: Look ahead for a flat area, such as a field, to land in.

Archie's problem was that, as far as he could see, there was no flat land, it was all mud and trenches and barbed wire. Any fields were miles away from the front.

The gasoline kept spraying out and now his clothes were soaked with it. Please, don't let it catch fire, he prayed silently.

His engine was off, which was a good thing. But it only needed one spark and he knew he'd go up in a ball of flames. His propeller was now the danger. Although the propeller had stuck after the engine failed, and seemed to be stuck in one position, he could see it wobbling slightly. Feverishly he hoped that the propeller had jammed. If it was still free, then it could start rotating of its own accord in the wind. As the propeller was locked in direct drive to the magneto of the engine, if the propeller began to turn, then the magneto would also turn, which would produce sparks. Archie's only hope was that the magneto had also been shattered, or was jammed solid.

Any of these situations would mean certain death for him because the fuel tank was at the front of the plane, close behind the propeller. If the propeller started up and fired the magneto, then the force of air generated by it would fan the flames straight at him.

During all the time he was thinking this he was coming down … down … down … doing his hardest to hold the plane level as the wind buffeted the wings and body.

"Glide!" he yelled aloud at the plane, heaving back on the joystick to stop the nose of the plane from going too far down, but not too hard because that could send the plane into a spin.

Down down he went… The ground below and in front of him was clearer now, coming up fast. So far the propeller hadn't moved. His luck was still holding … and then, to his horror, he saw the propeller shift slightly, and then begin to turn.

"No!!" he yelled aloud, and he waited for the sudden WHOOF of sparks from the magneto igniting the gasoline and the flames … but instead the plane just continued its descent, getting faster now as it neared the ground. The Red Baron's bullets must have smashed the magneto. At least, he hoped so. He tensed, waiting for any sound of sparks or small explosions that might signify fire. He was still too high to leap out of the plane and survive, but he decided he'd rather die from falling than being burnt to death.

Down and down he came, and now he was aware that the trenches and the barbed wire and the mud were getting nearer and nearer … men were shouting, shouts of anger and alarm, but no one was shooting at him. He was coming down behind his own lines. Providing the magneto didn't suddenly kick in to life, all he had to do was hold the plane level and hope it didn't fall apart as it hit the ground. With nowhere to land at speed and taxi, it meant just bringing it down where he could.

Suddenly everything was flashing up at him, flashing past at incredible speed, barbed wire, wooden posts, banks of mud. There was a sickening crunch as his undercarriage hit something, and then his left wing smashed into something else and just collapsed, the rigging falling apart, and the whole plane began to leap up into the air, and then to roll. He held onto the controls as tightly as he could, but then the plane gave a last massive jerk and Archie found the controls coming away in his hand, and then he was flying through the air, head over heels, and suddenly he hit a pool of water and began to sink.

As the thick, foul-smelling water closed over his head, the thought went through his mind: *Oh God, I survived the fall and now I'm going to drown.*

He pushed himself up to the surface and struck out for a wall of mud at one side. His hair and eyes were so wet with mud that he could barely see. His hands touched the wall of mud, and then his feet found some kind of footing beneath the water, and he began to push himself up.

"Here are you, mate!" called a voice. "I'll give you a hand!"

A soldier had appeared at the top of the wall of mud and he held out his hand to Archie.

Archie grasped it, and the soldier hauled him upwards, out of the way, dragging him, and Archie flopped over the top and rolled down the other side into more mud.

He was alive!

It took Archie two days to get back to his unit at the airfield at St Omer, hitching lifts on trucks. The first person he saw as he walked back into the Operations Hut was Buster, who burst into laughter.

"That's a fine welcome back!" complained Archie. "What's so funny?"

"I've decided to call you Lazarus," Buster chuckled. "Wasn't he the bloke who came back from the dead?"

"I wasn't dead," Archie pointed out.

"Yes, but you ought to have been," said Buster. "You're shot down from ten thousand feet…"

"I wasn't that high," Archie insisted. "Anyway, I was able to glide down."

"Your plane breaks up into pieces, and you're stuck in the middle of a ground battle between our boys and the Hun, shot and shell all around you, and you walk away from it!"

"I didn't exactly walk away," countered Archie. "I nearly drowned in a trench full of water."

"What I want to know is how you got out of it," said Derek. "So I know what to do if it ever happens to me."

"The first thing to do is be shot by a gentleman," said Archie. "One who shoots your engine and doesn't follow it up shooting you when you're on your way down, like some of the Hun swine."

"Von Richthofen," nodded Buster. "That's quite some tale: to be shot down by the Red Baron himself and live to tell the tale."

Archie looked around the hut and noticed a lot of new faces, with quite a few of them wearing different flying insignias.

"What's up?" he asked.

"We're being merged," said Derek. He gave a rueful sigh. "Afraid we're losing so many chaps we haven't got enough even to form a decent set of squadrons."

"They're good chaps, though," said Derek. "Canadians, mostly. Plus some new bugs just out from England."

Archie scanned the faces of the men sitting in the hut.

"Where's Wilson?" he asked.

There was an uncomfortable pause, and then Derek said: "He didn't make it."

Archie stared at him.

"Didn't…?"

"I'm afraid he wasn't as lucky as you, Archie," said Buster. "The Red Baron got him as well, but his crate fell apart in the air."

Although Buster was appearing to be flippant, Archie could see the tears in his eyes, and the way his lip trembled. Archie stood there, numb.

When they'd been training, Archie, Buster and Wilson had been inseparable, doing everything together, and having the best fun. They'd called themselves the Three Musketeers, one for all and all for one, and they'd meant it. Wilson had been engaged to be married, and the three of them had taken a vow that when the War was over they'd meet up together back in England and get royally sloshed the night before his wedding.

Now that would never happen.

"Gentlemen, take your seats!"

Squadron Leader Pierce had come into the room and taken his place at the front. The men took their seats. Archie was still in a state of shock and anger at Wilson's death. Pierce must have seen his feelings in his face and decided to try and stop him getting down about it, because he said: "Welcome back, Lieutenant Merton. Congratulations on finding your way back," then he added pointedly, "even if you did write off a perfectly good and very expensive plane!"

"With respect, sir, it was a German who wrote my plane off. I did my best to keep it intact. In fact, I was doing quite well until we hit the ground."

The other men laughed at this, breaking the sombre mood, which is what Archie guessed Pierce had been aiming for.

Pierce then went on to introduce the "new" members of the Unit, although it was obvious that most of them, especially the Canadians, were old hands. There was one new boy, though, obviously fresh out from England, and fresh in the business of war in the air. This became obvious when, after Pierce had finished the briefing and asked if there were any questions, he raised his hand.

"You have a question, Lieutenant Spriggs?" asked Pierce.

"Yes, sir," said Spriggs. "I wondered if there were any plans to issue us with parachutes?"

"It is not the policy of the RFC to give people an easy way out," replied Pierce sternly. "Parachutes are only issued to observers in balloons, in case their balloon gets shot down by the enemy. They have no other way of getting down except by parachute. You men, on the other hand, have been trained to fly your machine in all circumstances."

"Yes, sir, but say our plane catches fire. There's not a lot we can do with it if that happens."

"Then your job is to aim your plane at the enemy and take as many of them with you as you can," said Pierce. "Now, if there are no further questions…" And he said it in such a way to make sure that there wouldn't be any more. When there were no more questions, the order came: "Dismiss."

As the briefing broke up, Archie went across to the new boy, Lieutenant Spriggs, and offered his hand.

"Archie Merton," he introduced myself. "And don't let yourself be put out by Pierce having a go at you like that. It's a question all of us have asked at one time or another."

"Me, I'd like a parachute," said a friendly Canadian voice beside them. "But I guess the Top Brass are just too damned tight-fisted to spend the money."

Archie turned and saw a man who sounded like he was in his mid twenties, although with his sunken cheeks and his hair already beginning to turn grey, he looked much older. "Captain Arthur Roy Brown," he introduced himself. "From Ottawa. It looks as if we're going to be flying together."

Archie thrust out his hand and shook Brown's hand with genuine pleasure. Captain Brown was a legend among Allied fliers. With the average life expectancy of a pilot being barely two weeks, Brown had been flying combat since 1915, had shot down innumerable German planes, and had received the Distinguished Service Cross. His fighter plane with the maple leaf of Canada painted just above the circle of red, white and blue on its fuselage had become as familiar in the skies above the battlefield of the Somme as von Richthofen's red fighter.

"It will be a great pleasure," said Archie. "My name's Archie Merton."

"The man who was shot down by the Red Baron and lived to tell the tale," said Brown.

Archie thought about Wilson, and a vow of vengeance came to him.

"And I'm going to be the man who shoots down von Richthofen," he said grimly.

The next morning at 0715 hours, the whole squadron were assembled on the field: fourteen single-seater fighter planes, and six two-seaters. This was going to be a bombing raid, with the two-seaters dropping their ordnance on the Germans to try and make a crack in their lines. *One thing we can be sure of*, thought Archie, *once the Germans realize we're out in force, they'll be sending up their own planes, and that means the Red Baron and his Jasta. And this time, I'm going to make sure he goes down in flames!*

The morning seemed particularly chill, and Archie knew it would be even colder at 10,000 feet, so he'd made sure he was dressed to withstand the cold. He had on his leather flying jacket with its big fleecy collar, a woolly scarf, thick gloves, fleece-lined flying boots, and his leather flying cap.

At the whistle they "mounted up", clambering into the cockpits of their planes. At 0740 hours they started their engines. The six two-seaters, being slower, took off first and headed in a southerly direction, keeping behind the Allied lines for safety, waiting to rendezvous with their fighter escorts.

The two-seaters began their bombing of the German lines, dropping down low, the observer in the rear of the plane leaning out and sending the bombs hurtling down towards the ground. As they did so, Archie saw, in the distance, the German planes.

As they had planned, eight of the pilots had lifted up to 12,000 feet and headed in formation towards the oncoming enemy planes. The plan was to head the Germans off while the two-seaters continued with their bombing work, protected by the remaining six members of the squadron. As soon as the two-seaters had finished, they were to turn and head back home, the six escorts staying with them to protect them against any stray German who'd managed to get past Archie and the other escorts.

As he neared the approaching German planes, Archie felt a thrill of excitement as he recognized the bright red colour of one standing out: the Red Baron had come looking for more victims.

The planes from both sides began firing. It had become a standard tactic, firing a burst to try and make your opponent react, throw him off his track. But Archie had only one target in mind, and he headed for him now.

One of the German pilots saw the direction Archie was heading and turned and followed him, opening up with a burst of gunfire as he did so, but Archie caught the movement out of the corner of his eye and managed to turn aside at the last moment, and the line of tracer missed the front of his plane by inches.

He cautioned himself to be careful, not to let his desire to get von Richthofen blind him to the fact that all of the German squadron were superb pilots in their own right. Any one of them could shoot him down if he didn't keep his wits about him.

The air battle was already in full swing, the German planes hurtling this way and that, guns blazing, while the Allied planes ducked and dived and fired back, every man desperate to get an accurate, or at least lucky, shot in before his adversary could get a fix on him.

Two planes were already going down, both of them in flames, one British, leaving a trail of black smoke behind them in the air as they hurtled groundwards.

A German fired a burst at Archie, and he felt his machine shudder as his bullets hit the woodwork behind him, but he put his plane's nose down and went into a short dive, and then flew back up, turning as he did so, enough to bring him onto the German's tail. He fired off a burst and saw the German's tail fall to pieces, and the next second he sank like a stone, going into a spin, the wings whirling around like a spinning top.

Another German came at him, and this time he flew higher, with a quick upward glance first to make sure he wasn't on a collision course with anyone. There was one plane above him, bright red. Von Richthofen!

Unfortunately, the momentary jolt of realization that it was von Richthofen himself delayed his finger for just a fraction of a second too long from the trigger, and the German ace flipped neatly away from Archie's line of bullets, turning left, and then going higher. Archie followed him up to 15,000 feet. It was colder up here, much colder, and he was glad he had his sheepskin gloves on or his hands would have been too cold to operate the gun.

He fired off another burst, but again the Red Baron avoided his gunfire, this time wheeling to the right, Archie's bullets passing harmlessly beneath his left wing as it went up and he turned. Von Richthofen seemed to have some kind of sixth sense, as if he knew what Archie was going to do next.

Suddenly the Red Baron turned so sharply that Archie thought he was going to run into him head-on, and he pulled back on the joystick to lift up. Too late he heard the ack-ack-ack explosion of the German's guns, and he felt a searing pain in his right shoulder. The whole right side of his body went numb, but just for a second, and then the pain kicked in with a vengeance. Archie could feel his shirt inside his jacket starting to get wet around the shoulder and chest, and knew he'd been shot. A bullet had gone straight through his leather jacket. It hurt like hell. Already his right arm was starting to go numb, and every movement of his hand on the controls sent a jolt of pain through his upper body. He wondered how bad the wound was. How much blood had he lost already?

He was just trying to recover himself, regain control of his machine, when he saw von Richthofen coming back at him from the left-hand side, coming to finish him off.

Archie gritted his teeth against the pain and put his plane into a dive. He was just in time because a burst from von Richthofen's guns tore through the sky over his head as he dropped. If he'd delayed even by a second he'd have been riddled with bullets.

He saw the shadow of von Richthofen's plane spiral down from above him, and guessed he was intending to come in from behind. Immediately Archie went into a further dive to take him lower. As before, von Richthofen followed him down. He must have guessed he'd hit Archie, and maybe thought he'd lost enough blood to start losing consciousness. Archie began to spiral down, and then suddenly, abruptly, pulled the joystick back hard and soared up, heading straight into the Red Baron's flight path.

His manoeuvre caught von Richthofen by surprise and the German hastily turned sharply to avoid crashing. Although he fired off a burst, it was a reflex action because he was more concerned about getting out of Archie's way.

Archie was now above him, about 17,000 feet, and he was getting colder, which made handling his plane more difficult. The pain in his shoulder was spreading across his chest. He knew he couldn't hold out much longer; he had to do something to stop the loss of blood before he lost consciousness.

The chatter-chatter-chatter of rapid machine-gun fire from behind him told him that von Richthofen had recovered and was on his tail again, firing at him, trying to finish him off. Again, Archie put his plane's nose down and dived beneath the tracer of bullets, and turned, then turned quickly again to put himself on a level course with von Richthofen, heading straight for the German's plane broadside on, working the trigger as he did so … and to his shock, nothing happened. Archie knew he wasn't out of bullets. The firing mechanism had jammed!

Archie cursed. Here he was, in an air battle with a leading German ace. He was wounded, losing blood, and without working guns.

He watched the Red Baron circle above him, like a hunting eagle circling its prey, and then he dived, swooping towards Archie. And as he did, another fighter plane suddenly came out of nowhere, its guns blazing, and von Richthofen's plane seemed to erupt as bullets tore into it, ripping into the fabric of the fuselage and the cockpit.

The pilot flew past, waggling his wings as he did so, and Archie saw the maple leaf just above the red, white and blue on the fuselage.

Captain Arthur Roy Brown had just become the Ace of Aces.

April–November 1918

Manfred von Richtofen, the Red Baron, was the most famous fighter pilot of the First World War. He became a fighter pilot in 1916, and by the time of his death in 1918 he had shot down 80 Allied fighter planes. He and his squadron, Jasta 11 (known as The Flying Circus) became the most feared of all German aerial combat squadrons. He was killed in air combat on 21 April 1918, shot down by the Canadian pilot, Arthur Roy Brown.

By the end of the War, there were 5,128 Allied pilots still in service. Out of a total of 21,805, 9,378 had been killed or were missing, 7,245 had been wounded – a casualty rate of 76 per cent. The casualty rate for German flyers was: 5,853 killed; 7,302 wounded; 2,751 missing or taken prisoner.

Parachutes for single-seater planes were finally introduced on 16 September 1918.

Although the War continued across the globe, the decisive actions – the ones that would determine the outcome of the War – were taking place on the Western Front in France.

The announcement by President Wilson of the USA that a million American soldiers were being sent to bolster the Allies in France had a major impact. In July, the Germans began to retreat at Marne; and an Allied offensive at Amiens in August 1918 led to the collapse of the German Second Army. By late August, the Germans had been forced back to the Hindenburg Line – a series of defences built along Germany's border with northern and western France – which came under sustained attack during September, and was breached along its length and then cleared by Allied forces during October.

By the beginning of November the Germans accepted that the War in France had been lost and surrendered.

The Armistice to end the War was signed in a railway carriage at Rethondes in the Forest of Compiégne on 11 November, and thereafter 11.11.11 (11 a.m. on the 11 November – the 11th month) has been Remembrance Day, with the Sunday nearest to it known as Remembrance Sunday, the day on which the dead of the First World War, and all other wars, are remembered.

The last British fatality from enemy action before the Armistice went into effect was a cavalryman from C Troop 5th Royal Irish Lancers, George Edwin Ellison, shot by a sniper at Mons on 11 November. In one way, the cavalry had bookended the First World War: the first British shot of the War being fired by another cavalryman, Edward Thomas of the 4th Royal Irish Dragoons.

Homecoming

November 1918

"Make sure you tie the end of those flags tight! We don't want them falling down when he comes in!"

"Yes, Mam."

Thirteen-year-old Alice Sills had already made sure that the two ends of the banner, made up of small Union Flags, were tied tightly: one end to the hat stand in the hall, and the other to a nail in the wall on which hung a picture of Grandfather Sills.

Her brother, Jeb, was coming home. He'd gone away to war in 1915, when he was only seventeen, and the family hadn't seen him since. Other men had come home on leave during the War, but not Jeb. He'd been taken prisoner at the Battle of the Somme in 1916.

At first, they hadn't known whether he was alive or dead; so many of the Accrington Pals had died on that first day of the Somme, July 1916.

At first, no one in her street, or even in the whole of Accrington, would talk about it. It was only gradually, as weeks passed, that word about the number of casualties came through.

The Accrington Pals. A battalion formed in Accrington, Lancashire, made up of men who worked at the same factory, or lived in the same streets, or played for the same football teams.

Her dad had told her at the time there were lots and lots of these pals battalions being formed: the Burnley Pals, the Blackburn Pals, the Chorley Pals. And not just from Lancashire, but all over the country. Battalions where everyone knew one another, were friends who'd look after each other. And, like all the other pals battalions, the Accrington Pals had gone off to war.

First, to Egypt. Jeb had sent Alice postcards from Egypt with funny little messages and jokes on them. Alice had been ten, and for her, her brother Jeb was the brightest star of the Accrington Pals. Not only was he going off to be a soldier, he was funny and clever and he made her laugh, even when he was in Egypt. He sent her a postcard with a camel on it, and wrote "A picture of Mr Dickens", and that had made her laugh out loud. Mr Dickens was her teacher at school, and he'd been Jeb's teacher before; and he did look a bit like a camel with those big teeth of his sticking out at all angles.

Then Jeb had sent her a postcard saying, "We're being sent to …", but the rest of it had been blacked out by someone. Her dad told her it was a censor who'd done it.

"They have to make sure that the enemy don't find out what our lads are up to, lass," he'd told her. "So they go through the letters and stuff our blokes send home and make sure they don't give any information away that could help the enemy."

So the enemy never found out where Jeb was going to after he sent the postcard from Egypt, and neither did Alice.

Not at first.

She found out later.

The Accrington Pals had been sent from Egypt to France to the Western Front, which is what they called the place where the biggest battles were going on. That much Alice knew because they spoke about it in the shops and in the factories.

"I wonder what he'll look like?" Alice heard her mam ask her dad, her voice fearful.

"Shush, Nancy," said her dad sharply. "You'll frighten Alice!"

Why will I be frightened? Alice wondered to herself. *Have the Germans done something bad to Jeb?*

She'd seen some of the men who'd come back from the Front, from the trenches. Some of them had been gassed and were now blind. Some couldn't walk five steps without stopping to spit to clear their lungs of the muck that was in them, because of the gas.

Others had lost arms, or legs. Or, in the case of Johnny Pett from the next street, an arm and both legs, and people whispered to one another that it would have been better if he'd died.

They're cruel, thought Alice. *I don't care what Jeb looks like now, he's my brother and I love him.*

On the first day of the Battle of the Somme, 1 July 1916, along with loads of other Allied troops, the Accrington Pals had gone into battle, 700 of them. From accounts Alice heard later, the attack lasted barely half an hour. At the end of it, 235 of the Accrington Pals were dead and another 350 wounded – 585 casualties out of 700.

They said that Jeb was one of the lucky ones; he was captured by the Germans and taken prisoner. But spending three years in a German prisoner-of-war camp didn't seem lucky to Alice.

Alice remembered the bad feeling in Accrington when the news got back. More than bad feeling: a rumour came that only seven men had survived from the 700 of the Accrington Pals, and people had been so angry they'd gone round to the house where the Mayor of Accrington lived. And there was talk of people wanting to drag him out of his house and hang him from a lamppost, because it was the Mayor who'd come up with the idea of a battalion called the Accrington Pals, and he'd encouraged all the young men to join it. The police had to intervene and save the Mayor from the angry mob: mothers and fathers and brothers and sisters and wives of the men who'd been lost.

Later, the Mayor issued a statement saying that none of it was his fault, he was only carrying out orders from Lord Kitchener, the War Minister, to raise a battalion. Of course, he was safe in laying the blame on Kitchener, because Kitchener was dead, killed in 1916 when the ship he was in hit a floating mine off the coast near Scotland.

But the War was over now, and Jeb was coming home.

What would he look like? Alice wondered.

There'd been some letters from him when he was in the prisoner-of-war camp. Prisoners were allowed to write letters home, and get them back. They were also allowed to get parcels from home, and

Alice's mam had sent him some food and some warm clothes, but they were never sure if he got all of them, because his letters didn't always mention them.

Jeb didn't write for a long while after that day in July, which is why they all thought at first he was dead.

The War Office said he wasn't, that they had no note of him having been killed or wounded, but everyone knew that some of the men who were killed were just left lying where they fell and their bodies weren't recovered, and no one knew they'd died.

Alice had prayed every night for God to send Jeb home after the news came through about that day on the Somme, or at least for God to send them news about him: if he was alive.

But God never said. And nor did the War Office. That was why that first letter that came from Jeb late in July was so special. He told them he'd been taken prisoner but he was all right.

A few months later came another letter from him, saying he was still all right, but not much more.

Alice wrote to him, and her mam put it in the same envelope as her own letter to Jeb, but Jeb never wrote back, which is why Alice wondered if Jeb had got her letter.

A few months later he did write again, but not to her, and that hurt her. Her mam showed her Jeb's letter. There were no jokes in it. All he said was he was all right and that it was cold where he was, but he was getting on with things and he hoped the War would be over soon so he could see them all again.

As time passed, the gaps between Jeb's letters became longer: two months, three, then six. Alice guessed it was because he had nothing new to say, but she wished he'd write, just so they'd know he was still alive.

And then came the Armistice. And soon after came a letter from Jeb. He was being released. He was coming home.

When? That was the question uppermost in her mind, but no one seemed to know. Her dad had contacted the War Office, but they didn't know. They said there were so many men coming home that they couldn't keep track of them all.

How was Jeb going to get home? asked Alice.

Again, the War Office didn't know that. There were boats and lorries and buses and trains. Some ticket vouchers had been issued, as well, but they didn't know if Jeb Sills had one. Once again, they told her dad: *There are so many men coming home we can't keep track of them all.*

And so Mam had started decorating the house ready for Jeb's return as soon as she got the letter from him, with bunting and flags and a home-made sign – that Alice had made – that said WELCOME HOME JEB.

That had been over a week ago, and still there had been no sign of Jeb, or any word from him. *Where was he?* Alice wondered. *Had he even managed to leave the prisoner-of-war camp? He wouldn't have any money, so how would he be able to get a boat and a bus home? Had he been issued with a ticket voucher?*

Alice had a vision of Jeb walking home, starting in Germany, and walking right across Belgium and France – she'd checked all these places on her school atlas, so she knew where they were – to the French coast. But how could he get across the water without any money? They said there were troopships bringing soldiers home from France, but Jeb wasn't a soldier any more, he was a prisoner of war. Would someone give him a lift on a fishing boat?

In the meantime, while they waited, Mam insisted they keep the Welcome Home decorations fresh, changing the bunting, moving the welcome signs to a different place, re-tying the string of Union Flags, as Alice had just done, to make sure they wouldn't fall down.

By six o'clock that evening there was still no sign of Jeb, just as there hadn't been for a week now. *Where was he?* worried Alice. *Was he really on his way home, or had something happened to him?*

Dad looked at the clock on the mantelpiece and gave a weary sigh. Mam had put off getting supper ready, waiting in case Jeb arrived.

"Reckon he won't be here today," he said. "Maybe tomorrow. Better get supper."

Reluctantly, Mam went into the kitchen and began to prepare potatoes and cabbage to go with the stew she'd had cooking on the stove all day, and the day before. Alice went to help her peel the potatoes.

"Maybe he got held up in France," said Mam. "It can't be easy getting across the Channel."

But Alice could tell from the way her mam hunched over as she cut up the cabbage that she was worried. Over a week and still no word.

Mam was just about to put the potatoes on to boil, when there was a knock at the front door. Immediately, Mam stopped and looked at Alice.

"That could be him!" she said breathlessly.

"Only one way to find out," said Dad, and he walked into the hallway and opened the door as Alice and her mam crowded anxiously behind him.

At first, Alice didn't recognize the man who stood there. For one thing, Jeb would be twenty. The thin man standing on the doorstep looked much older.

And he *was* thin. Jeb had been a well-built young man, broad-shouldered, thick neck. The man who stood there looked like pictures Alice had been shown at Sunday School of poor children in Africa who were starving; his head wasn't so much a head as a skull with skin stretched over it.

But it was Jeb. It was the ears that gave him away. They'd always stuck out sideways, and they were sticking out now.

"Jeb!"

Mam pushed past Dad and Alice and rushed to the young man, wrapping her arms around him, hauling him over the doorstep into the house.

"Oh, my boy! My boy!"

But he isn't a boy, thought Alice as she looked on, and the realization hurt her. The brother who'd made her laugh and had been the life of the street had gone. Now there was an old-young man standing awkwardly as their mam embraced him.

"Hey up, Nancy," said Dad. "Let the rest of us get a look in!"

Reluctantly, Mam let Jeb go and he stepped forward, and Dad took his hand and shook it.

"Welcome home, son," he said.

In answer, Jeb just nodded. Then he turned and saw Alice, and frowned.

"Is that our Alice?" he asked.

"Yes," said Alice, and she moved nearer to this thin, haggard man. She wanted to run to him and throw her arms around him, as her mam had done, but somehow it didn't seem right. *He* didn't seem right. He wasn't the Jeb who'd left home.

"Yes," said Alice. "That's me all right."

"You've grown," said Jeb.

"I'm just making supper," said Mam. "Come in and eat. You look like it's been a long time since you've had a decent meal."

"Thanks, Mam, but I'm not hungry," said Jeb.

Dad and Mam looked at the rake-like man, shocked.

"Not hungry!" echoed Dad.

"Not at the moment," said Jeb. "I just want to put my head down. I haven't had a lot of sleep, and it's taken me a long time to get here. Is my room still the same?"

"Of course!" said Mam indignantly. "What else would we have done with it? But surely you'll want a cup of tea? You've only just got home, and we haven't seen you for three years."

Jeb hesitated, then he forced a smile and nodded.

"Yes," he said. "Sorry. A cup of tea would be perfect."

"Right. If you go into the parlour with your dad I'll make some and bring it in."

The parlour was the front room, and used for best occasions: weddings and funerals.

"Actually, I'd rather go into the kitchen," said Jeb. He indicated his clothes, and for the first time Alice realized how dirty and ragged and stained they were. "I'm not ready for the parlour yet."

"You don't have to dress up for the parlour," said Dad, although Alice reflected that people did. The parlour was special, kept clean and polished, and only best clothes were to be worn by those using it. "But if you feel happier in the kitchen, so be it."

And so the four of them went into the kitchen, where Mam bustled about making a pot of tea. Dad gave Jeb the best chair, the old upright wooden armchair which he usually sat in.

There are so many questions, thought Alice. *I want to know what life was like in the prisoner-of-war camp. How did you get here? How did you get so thin?*

Alice could see that Dad was also bursting to ask the same questions, but Dad's probing just received a sort of sad forced smile as Jeb sipped at his tea. Mam filled in the silence with talk of people in the streets round about that Jeb used to know, but then she stopped when she realized that a lot of them were the families of those who died at the Somme, and they all noticed Jeb wince when certain names were mentioned.

After a while, with Jeb sitting there like a strange old-young man in awkward silence, Dad said: "Well, I think it's time you did what you suggested and took a nap. You've had a long journey, but you're home now, and we can talk all we like tomorrow."

237

"Aye," nodded Jeb, and he got up and gave them all a weak smile, and then he left the kitchen and they heard him clomp up the stairs to his old room.

After he'd gone, Dad and Mam sat in an awkward silence for a moment, before Dad said: "Well, he's home, and that's a blessing." And Mam said it was a blessing, and everything would be all right now. But Alice knew it wasn't all right, and she worried that maybe it would never be all right. Jeb had left, and a stranger had come home, a stranger that none of them knew how to deal with.

They heard the creaking of the floorboards above them as Jeb settled down on his bed. Then, while Mam busied herself once more with putting the supper on, Dad suggested a hand or two of cards for him and Alice. Alice knew it was only being done as a way of avoiding talking about Jeb, or what would happen now, and she joined in, but she knew she was only putting off the time when she'd be asking Jeb the questions that filled her mind. What had happened to her brother?

They played cards until supper was ready. Then they played a few more hands of cards; and then Alice said goodnight to her parents and went upstairs to bed.

She hesitated as she reached the door of her brother's room, and found herself listening; and then really listening. There was a sound from inside the room she'd never heard before, a man crying.

Before she could stop herself, she tapped at the door with her knuckles, and then cursed herself for doing it. He needed to be private.

But she had to know, she'd been carrying the question for over three years: *What had happened?*

"Yes?" came Jeb's voice from inside.

Alice turned the handle and pushed the door open.

Jeb was sitting on the bed, still dressed in the same raggedy stained clothes he'd arrived in. Alice came in, shut the door, then went to the bed and sat down next to her brother.

"I was worried about you," she said.

The old Jeb would have said: "I'm all right", or something similar; but this Jeb didn't. Instead, he closed his eyes, and Alice saw the tears rolling down his cheeks. She didn't say anything. Instead, she reached out and took one of his hands and squeezed it, and held it; and Jeb began to sob, deep heartfelt sobs, as if a whole war's worth of tears that had been held back was now pouring out.

They sat like that for a long time: Jeb crying, and Alice holding his hand, until finally Jeb stopped crying and opened his eyes. He took a long deep breath, then another, and wiped his eyes with the back of his free hand.

"It was bad?" asked Alice, nervously, afraid that asking the question would just make him shut up.

He nodded.

"It was bad," he said, "but now it's worse in some ways."

"Worse?" asked Alice, puzzled. "Worse than the War?"

"No, nothing's worse than the War," said Jeb. "But, now..." And he stopped. He turned to Alice and asked: "You remember when I went away to war?"

Alice nodded.

"The Accrington Pals," he said, and his voice was a mixture of sadness and bitterness. "At first it was a laugh, although we knew it was serious business we were on. The training was tough, but not as hard as working at Battleys. And we younger ones handled it better than the older blokes."

"You sent me postcards," said Alice. "I've still got the ones you sent me from Egypt."

"Egypt," nodded Jeb, and he gave the ghost of a smile. "Egypt was all right. Hot, and with flies everywhere, but all right. It was France that did for us."

He gave a heavy sigh.

"First of July 1916. The first day of the Battle of the Somme. The Accrington Pals all together, ready to fight. Seven hundred of us went into the attack on that first day. You know what happened?"

Alice nodded.

"Most got killed or wounded," she said. "We didn't know if you were alive until a long time after."

"I was one of the lucky ones," said Jeb, but there was deep bitterness his voice.

"How did you get captured?"

Jeb sat silent, not looking at her, his memory filled with that dreadful day, then he said: "I made it all the way to the German lines, and when

I looked round, there was no one with me. All the others were lying behind me, dead. Then this German hit me in the face with his rifle and knocked me out. I found out later he only did it because he was out of ammunition, otherwise he'd have shot me dead."

He fell silent again, and Alice could see that he was recalling the moment when he reached the German lines and realized he was all alone, and her heart went out to him. He would have been seventeen, and alone, surrounded by hundreds of enemies, with his comrades dead. Alice wanted to put her arms around him, hug him and tell him it was going to be all right. But she knew it wasn't, so she didn't. She just sat there and watched him as he talked; not so much talking to her as talking to himself to dredge up the memories, face them, live with them.

"Was it … was it bad in the prisoner-of-war camp?" she asked.

"The food was," said Jeb. "We got food parcels from the Red Cross and from home, which was good, but sometimes the guards used to steal them before we got them. We found out that's because the guards didn't get much better food than we got in the camps. A lot of the meat was rotten. Same with the vegetables. We had a lot of soup. And acorns. Stewed acorns. Ground-up acorns turned into bread."

"What did it taste like?" asked Alice.

"Rotten," said Jeb. "A lot of the blokes got sick. The trouble was there weren't enough latrines, and when blokes got sick…" He didn't finish, but the memory was there on his face. "There was a lot of disease. Blokes died." Again, he fell silent, then he said: "Seven hundred men went away. Six hundred got shot. I guess the others who didn't get taken prisoner, like happened to me, went on to fight again. But at the end, of the forty of us from the Accrington Pals who were in the prisoner-of-war camp, I was the only one alive at the end. And I feel bad about that."

"Why?" asked Alice, puzzled.

"Because the others died."

"But that wasn't your fault," said Alice.

"I know. But I can see it in the faces of the women who lost their sons or their husbands, and I can tell they're thinking: 'Why are you alive while my son is dead?' And they hate me."

"No they don't," said Alice.

"Yes they do," insisted Jeb. "You can't feel it the way I do. You don't know that look I get from them. That's why I didn't come here earlier when I arrived home."

"You were here?" asked Alice, surprised.

Jeb nodded.

"This morning," he said. "I got a bus from Manchester which landed me at the bus station where I had to change to get my bus home. And there they all were, families, especially women, who'd lost someone from the Accrington Pals. They saw me sitting there, waiting for the bus, and I could tell that quite a few of them recognized me. I even heard one of them whisper to someone: 'That's Jeb Sills who got taken prisoner.'

"In the end I couldn't stand it and I gave up waiting for the bus and decided to walk home. But the nearer I got to home the more people I saw who knew me from the old days. And not one of them came up to me and said they were glad to see me, or asked how I was. All I could see in their faces was the same angry look: 'Why are you alive while mine is dead?'

"I've spent more than three years in the worst conditions you could ever imagine. I've seen my mates die around me, both in war and in the prison camp, but people look at me as if I'm the guilty one.

"So, I turned round and walked away."

"Away from home?"

Jeb nodded.

"I walked back to the edge of town, to Henry's Field, and I put myself under a hedge where no one could see me, and I waited there until it got dark enough that I could walk home without people seeing me and recognizing me. But all I've done is put it off till tomorrow. Tomorrow, when I go out, those same looks will be there. And then they'll look away from me."

"They're not looking at you like that, Jeb," said Alice. "It's just that they don't know what to say to you. That's the only reason they look away."

Jeb shook his head.

"The War was bad, but at least we knew where we stood. Now, no one knows what to do with those of us who survived. Do they feel grateful? No. They keep that for the ones who died. The ones of us who lived, we're a reminder of the bad things that happened."

Then he took a deep breath and his grip on her hand tightened as he said, with a fierce emotion, the first he'd shown since he'd walked through the front door: "But there's one good thing that'll come out of all this, Alice. Out of all this death and misery. Every family here's lost someone in this war. And in every town in Britain. The same in Germany and France, and all over. Everyone's grieving for someone, and they'll fight like anything to stop it from happening again. No one will want their kids to have that kind of suffering. Trust me, because of all that's happened, there won't be another war like this!"

Epilogue: Peace ... and war again

The global conflict between 1914 and 1918 was first known as the Great War, also known as the War To End Wars because of the mass slaughter. The casualty rates on the Western Front alone were enormous:

Germany: 1,808,543 dead; 4,247,143 wounded.

France: 1,385,300 dead; 3,614,700 wounded.

British Empire troops: 947,023 dead; 2,313,558 wounded.

USA: 115,600 dead; 210,216 wounded. (But the US didn't enter the War until 1917.)

Total: 4,256,466 dead; 10,385,617 wounded; 14,642,145 total casualties.

It was not called World War I or the First World War until the Second World War began. This was because no one could imagine, after the carnage and the millions of deaths, that any Government or people would allow their rulers to ever again involve them in a war of such awful magnitude. Yet that is exactly what happened just 21 years later, in 1939, and in living memory of the men who had survived the First World War, and now took their countries once more into a global conflict. With the Second World War, the countries of the world found themselves once again in a brutal conflict that spread across every continent of the world: Europe, Africa, Asia, North and South America, Australasia and the Pacific.

How did this happen?

Historians believe there were two reasons for this, both of which have their root causes in 1918.

The first was the terms of the Treaty of Versailles, the peace treaty which ended the First World War. Many believed the terms punished Germany so harshly that there was no way the country could recover economically. Under the terms of the treaty, Germany lost about 13.5 per cent of its 1914 territory (along with about 7 million people), about 13 per cent of its economic resources, and all of its overseas territories. Germany also had to pay heavy compensation to all the countries on the winning side.

The German Kaiser (its king), Wilhelm, was forced to abdicate, and the monarchy was replaced by a republic. Any union between Germany and Austria was also forbidden.

To prevent the rise of Germany as a military power, the German Army was limited to 100,000 men. Conscription was banned, as was heavy artillery, tanks, aircraft and airships. The German Navy was restricted to vessels of under 10,000 tons, and was forbidden to use submarines or aircraft. (However, because no time limit was set for imposing these restrictions, Adolf Hitler was able to ignore them and claim he was not in violation of the terms.)

The French were the driving force behind these conditions imposed on Germany. They saw the terms as both a punishment and also a way of preventing Germany from attacking them again.

Some British politicians feared that German resentment of their harsh economic situation could lead them to react against it and seek revenge. Many historians believe these politicians were proved right; because ten years later the economic situation in Germany was so bad that when a new National Socialist (Nazi) leader, Adolf Hitler, a former soldier, came to prominence and promised an end to the country's economic misery, many Germans welcomed him with open arms and gave him their support.

The second reason why the Second World War's roots lay in the time of the First World War was the Russian Revolution of 1918. Following the overthrow and murder of the Russian tsar and his family by Bolsheviks, Russia became a Soviet Republic, and by the 1930s it was one of the most powerful countries in the world, with ambitions to expand its empire. Adolf Hitler and the Nazis were fiercely opposed to Communism and saw Russia as their main enemy; although at first the two countries signed an agreement, the German-Soviet Pact. This was political protection on both sides, neither country wanting to go to war with the other (although they eventually did, with Russia siding with the Allies during the Second World War).

Germany and Russia weren't alone in battling to overturn harsh economic situations. Throughout the rest of Europe, and in America, the cost of the War had brought financial disaster to many. The result was a rise in both Fascism and Communism as the two political ideals battled for supremacy, and sought support from the people who were worst affected by the crippling financial aftermath of the War.

In other words: the Second World War came about because of a worldwide economic crisis, a desire to blame someone for it, and a belief in a rich and strong destiny.

Revenge, blame, power and money.

A lesson from history that still seems as relevant today as it did in 1918.